**CLAIMING A LIFE OF PURPOSE, PASSION, & PROSPERITY**

For more information or to contact the author please visit:

***www.crystaliberger.com***
***www.cbinspires.com***

Editor: **AMARI YARBROUGH**

Cover Photo: **KYLE POMPEY**

Cover Design: **ELEVATE BRANDING, INC.**

Follow on Twitter: @crystaliberger OR @cbinspires
Follow on Instagram: @cbinspires

# ENDORSEMENTS

"**Crystal** is an accomplished media professional and has used her experience to provide inspiration in a format that people can use and have time for. *Be Extraodinary* takes some of the most inspirational and motivational quotes of our time, organizes them according to our needs and provides them in short meaningful bites easily digestible by the heart and mind. Open to any page for your daily nourishment!"

-**Michael Houlihan** and **Bonnie Harvey**, New York Times Bestselling Authors of *The Barefoot Spirit, How Hardship, Hustle, and Heart Built America's #1 Wine Brand*.

"We all want to be happy. To reach our own potential. To be our best selves. ***Be Extraordinary*** helps show the way to achieve our best potential, and to be truly happy as we do. Crystal Berger's insights are right on target. And ***Be Extraordinary*** is a useful reference guide as we strive to be truly Extraordinary."

-**Lis Wiehl**, Fox News Legal Analyst, and New York Times best-selling author.

"Incredible! This amazing book is a treasure chest of inspiration, encouragement and love. **Crystal Berger** has done a wonderful job with creating a one stop shop for daily inspiration. Ms. Berger's love and passion for her community, family and our youth shows in this book. What a gift to all who needs a daily boost."

-**Meredith Lilly**, Esq., Political Strategist and Presidential Appointee Obama Administration.

# AUTHOR'S NOTE

It was a typically humid mid-July Saturday morning in Jersey when I woke up feeling contrastingly cold despite the sweat that had formed underneath my tightly pulled hair scarf overnight. It was beautiful outside in the sense that the sun was shining and I had been given another opportunity to do things better than I had done the day before; however, inside I felt so ugly. As I got up to start my morning physical transformation into the cheery disposition and likeable black girl at FOX News, I paused at my reflection in the mirror. Then they came. *They* were the demons of doubt that lived within me and brought up questions like, "Where is my life headed? Will things get better? Why don't I feel as pretty as everyone tells me I am?" and the worse one of them all, "Why don't you just checkout of life now?"

You see, from the outside, it seemed I had it all together—being aesthetically beautiful to most; the exterior appearance of intelligence and what society labels as a form of career success. But for me, waking up in the morning was becoming more and more daunting. The self-induced pressure of having to always be *on*—weave in place, the right SPANX to camouflage or slim my unsightly midsection under a no-name dress over my awkward six-foot tall frame. Using MAC concealer to hide three years of blemishes (what I call "stress wounds") from living a lonely life in New York did very little to cover the spiritual wounds I harbored internally.

Many days I'd wake up with numbness in my hands and feet and stiffness in my arms and neck and today was no different. I even struggled to grab the composition notebook where I would write these words that you are reading on this page. Although I was truly blessed with my health and opportunities, I struggled with loneliness, completion, and decades of insecurities. I was now thirty-five and wanting a family more so than a thriving career that I had been chasing for most of my adult life. I was in a city that I hated with no true friends, no family, and no prospects for real love. I was living in an 800-square foot apartment that I was ashamed to call home, yet, it was the only housing that my credit and income would allow. I was working for a media conglomerate where I felt isolated and sometimes bitter. The journey to achieving my dream was met with challenges, disappointments, and lots of uncertainty. Most days I just couldn't embrace that my glass was half full and that God was preparing me for something greater than me.

My journey to God's call from my life has come with much doubt, disappointment, and personal sacrifice. Not a day has gone by that I didn't need God's unchanging hand to lead me to the light of day. It's with those thoughts and prayers that I have the strength and the motivation to draft this book. When I turned through the pages of a journal that I've kept since I was fifteen-years-old, I realized that everything I had experienced in this life had been not about me, but the life lessons that I was created to bestow upon others. In reading how far I have come and the life that God spoke through me, even in times of uncertainty, I began to see the real light.

The real light was the light that had dimmed within me as I did my daily pity parties. I focused more and more on God's word and began to understand that life is truly about the process of getting to the destination and not the goal that is achieved in the end.

God works on us so that we can truly identify what we were created on this earth to do; our PURPOSE. He then takes us on a journey of PURPOSE that truly extracts our PASSION. We are then made to push so hard, even during the toughest times in life, to reach the point where we can serve and bless others. This is the PROSPERITY phase. I was once told that, "We are blessed to be a blessing." God will only have you go through it all in order to achieve the goal; so you can one day be of service to someone or many. I pray that this book helps motivate you to get started, to stick with and/ or complete God's calling and destination for your life.

Remember, I am no expert, preacher, or trained coach, but I am a living testimony of God's grace, mercy and favor. I'm simply an inner city girl from West Baltimore who has been able to shake the hands of world leaders, civil rights activists, Super Bowl MVPs, and various other agents of change because of God's hands on my life. I am an example of when you stay faithful and true to His vision "for NO thing is impossible with God" ~Luke 1:37. I'm possible because impossible does not exist in my world. I look forward to imparting this modern motivation to those who are living a life of purpose, passion and prosperity in today's nontraditional world.

# INTRODUCTION

In *Be Extraordinary*, I'll share the Top 25 ***Tips, Affirmations,*** and ***(#)Hashtags*** that I wish someone would have shared with me before taking a journey of low self-esteem, depression, abuse, and personal disappointments. These 25 tips will change your perception of **YOU**. 25 *Life Lessons* that will allow you to make better decisions and 25 ***(#)Hashtags*** that you can share with the world that will allow you to ultimately change your journey. Apply these tips daily, meditate on the scriptures provided to keep you rooted in faith, and keep these tips with you on note cards, in a journal; but more importantly keep them in your heart.

# *PURPOSE* in your Personal Life

Discovering purpose for your life is a journey; there is a divine order to it all.

**T**RUST yourself enough to know who you are and develop a sound SELF ESTEEM. This will allow you to love yourself enough to see the BEAUTY that you possess. Loving who you are opens you up to a purposeful life that develops into divine INTUITION; the kind of intuition that creates a strong FAITH in someone or something bigger than yourself. Ultimately, you'll start WINNING despite the situation because you have a unique UNDERSTANDING that lends itself to OPENNESS about your flaws and imperfections. You will learn how to FORGIVE yourself and others for not seeing or valuing who you are purposed to be/become. Learning to forgive yourself and others will allow you to make PEACE with every extraordinary thing that's happening in and around you.

Figuring out your PURPOSE in this life is not complicated. What is complicated is the amount of time we spend second guessing, questioning, and talking ourselves out of our purpose. Just like I use to look in the mirror and spend hours dissecting all the flaws instead of embracing these imperfections as works in progress. We spend a lot of time doing what's safe, what's predictable, and what others think we should do when in actuality we should simply do what we love. All of us are bestowed an innate talent; however, most of us immerse ourselves in the talents of others, wishing we had what they had. The longer we yearn for our brother or sisters' ability and ignore our own, the longer we stay void our purpose. When living and fulfilling your purpose, the process should feel organic; natural. Nothing should feel forced, contrived, or manipulated if your true purpose is being lived.

KNOW WHO YOU ARE (**Trust**)
TAKE AT GOOD LOOK AT YOURSELF (**Self Esteem**)
LOVE YOURSELF (**Beauty**)
IDENTIFY YOUR GIFT (**Possibilities**)
GO WITH YOUR GUT (**Intuition**)
STEP OUT OF YOUR BOX (**Faith**)
SURVIVE THE NEGATIVE SITUATION (**Winning**)
LEARN TO LISTEN (**Understanding**)
ACCEPT THAT YOU ARE A WORK IN PROGRESS (**Openness**)
FORGIVENESS IS FREEDOM (**Forgiveness**)
LET IT BE WHAT IT IS (**Peace**)

# *PASSION* in your Professional Life

Once you've discovered why you were created—
your purpose, you will develop the passion to
pursue your dreams. The process can be met with
lots of disappointments, adversities and trials,
but there are things that can be put into place
to ensure your journey of purpose is met with
excitement, joy and passion.

**F**irst, you must get a strong SUPPORT system in place that will assist you in your COMMITMENT to pursuing your purpose. The level of DEDICATION that it will take to being purposeful takes INITIATIVE and you can't be crippled by FEAR. Allow your TALENTS to drive your FOCUS. The kind of focus that makes you want to KNOW enough to be the UNDERDOG that stares ADVERSITY in the face with unshakeable **passion**.

**Passion**. It's one of those words that I had to say over and over again before I fully felt its true meaning. Most of us only associate passion with the feeling of intimacy, which it rightfully applies. The bond between two people whether fraternal or maternal is a feeling like none other. However, authentic passion reaches far past the physical. By definition, passion is that very strong, barely controllable emotion that we feel be it for a person, place, or thing. But for me, passion reaches even further as it is the driving force that not only wakes me up; it makes me want to get it done and never quit. When you navigate through your journey, your passion will help you overcome obstacles, face your fears, and achieve the greatest heights of your life.

GET YOUR CREW (**Support**)
DEVELOP YOUR GREATNESS (**Commitment**)
CONSISTENCY IS KEY (**Dedication**)
MAKE IT HAPPEN (**Initiative**)
FACE "IT" WITH FLARE (**Fear**)
MAKE PEOPLE WANT KNOW YOU (**Talent**)
BE "IN" IT, BUT NOT "OF" IT (**Focus**)
KNOW YOUR BOUNDARIES (**Knowledge**)
NO NEGATIVITY (**Underdog**)
SHAKE THOSE HATERS OFF (**Adversity**)

# *PROSPERITY* in your Philanthropic Life

Remember that purposeful passion will lead to personal and professional prosperity.

**B**efore you can ever prosper, you have to develop a grand UNDERSTANDING of why things have happened on your journey. This understanding will lead to a sense of CLOSURE that makes you want to commit to being of SERVICE to others. Committing to help others will bring you the kind of JOY that helps you stay focused on being EXTRAORDINARY.

Once you identify your purpose and you are working passionately towards your goals you will start to yield results also known as PROSPERITY. After all, your positive seeds have been planted and sewn; your harvest will reap in ways that you would have never thought possible. Not only will you see these results in your life but in those around you. If you are working with the right heart and soul in mind you will notice the attitudes and spirits of those in your company begin to take on a positive form. Being extraordinary in your service to others will lead to prosperity in all areas of your life.

DON'T RESENT YOUR SITUATION (**Understanding**)
LEARN TO SAY GOOD BYE OR GO HOME (**Closure**)
GET INVOLVED (**Service**)
DO IT WITH A SMILE (**Perspective**)
BE GOOD TO YOU (**Joy**)
BONUS: F.O.C.U.S.
BONUS: BE EXTRAORDINARY

# The *PURPOSE* Affirmations

# #KnowU

< 140: Embrace imperfections; we're all perfectly imperfect.

(53 Characters)

# #KnowU

**A**s a little girl, I was very thin, but assumed by the time puberty hit I would "fill" out. I looked forward to becoming what I saw the other girls of my West Baltimore neighborhood grow into. I hoped to one day fill out a full black body suit the way Salt-N-Pepa did in Push It. However, my long arms and long legs set against an even longer frame and what my friends would call a "pancake" behind would not fulfill my dreams of thickness—I was never destined to be featured in a LL Cool J or Sir Mix A Lot video. The brothers who I quietly sought to gain the attention and admiration of made fun of my shape and called me average. Without thick thighs to fill out a nice pair of leather riding boots or wide hips placed in a pair of stonewash Guess jeans I felt nothing short of inadequate. I had let someone else's perception define me. When I looked in the mirror I didn't see my Crystal; I saw other people's Crystal. I never knew that I had the prettiest shaped almond eyes and the brightest smile with dimples—some now say I was kissed by God on my cheeks.

Don't fault yourself for being something that you're not because you're what you're supposed to be. Accept what God gave you and celebrate it. If you're tall and skinny, work those legs. If your hair is kinky, rock those double-strand twists; as a matter of fact, get hot pink highlights and celebrate your full, thick, colorful locks.

**AFFIRMATION:** I am who GOD wanted me to be and I ABSOLUTELY love being me.

# #TheManInTheMirror

< 140: Introspection yields reflection which molds into perfection.

(60 characters)

# #TheManInTheMirror

Life can seem unforgiving at times. What can be even more unforgiving are our personal critiques of our external aesthetics. You may have had the awful experience of having been abused as a child. Your skin might be too pale, too freckled, too rough, or too dark. You may feel like you were treated unfairly by the people you loved the most. You may hate your tightly coiled hair or knocked-knees. You may not understand the eclectic mix of nationalities that make up you. But just take a moment to take a really good look at yourself. Snatch your inventory list and then tear it up. Burn the entire list of 'unfavorables' that weigh down the baggage that you're carrying. Then start from scratch, with a new list highlighting all the positive things that are on the shelf. Do you have the darkest skin of anyone else, the kind that shines in the sun? Do you have the widest hips of all the women, the kind that births multiple lives at once? Do you have the ability to speak articulately which allows people to take notice when you open your mouth? Point out the positives and focus on them. Remind yourself of all the good things you see staring back at you. Dig as deep as you can and learn to love what you've uncovered.

**AFFIRMATION**: I embrace the good and learn from the bad because I am a collection of all things perfect or not.

# #LoveU

< 140: Happiness is contagious; go viral.

(34 characters)

# #LoveU

I used to always look for people to love me. I searched for outside things to define my significance in the world. As a little girl, I was a daddy's girl. At 7, my love for myself left when my parents' divorce papers were filed. I tried finding happiness in guys, in overachieving and in accumulation of things. I masked a lack of self-love with a pretty smile and outward success. I even believed my external personas of happiness, until one day I looked in the mirror and realized I didn't love the person who was looking back at me. Not the outward person, but the hurt and broken person who I felt connecting with my own eyes in the mirror. I was a lost soul searching for happiness in others when all along what I was looking for was within me.

You hold the key to your own self-love. Pay close attention to the content of your character. Make sure you acknowledge the beautiful things that make you—YOU. Build yourself up, explore your gifts, and find that place of peace and happiness within yourself. Remember to be patient with yourself; remember to be kind to yourself. Never judge yourself, don't envy others, and don't hold yourself accountable for the things that you've already sought forgiveness for in your life. Always allow the love for you to prevail, even when times are tough.

**AFFIRMATION:** I love me, every imperfection, every unique trait, every beautiful thing about me, I simply love.

# #IDYourGift

< 140: Talent unused will be passed on to the next.

(37 characters)

# #IDYourGift

**A** lot of people spend their entire lives ignoring their gift and true passion. They settle into lives that make them grow angry and bitter with the world. Don't take your gift for granted. You know what you're good at and you know what you're great at in life. Follow the thing that is great. Allow your gift to open up the doors of infinite happiness in your life. Don't let people convince you to settle on what's safe in life. Take the risk and embrace the amazing. Look inside yourself to discover your gift and then get started on unwrapping your 'present' for the world to experience.

**AFFIRMATION:** I have a great gift inside of me. I am talented and created to do something uniquely special. My talent will lead me to my destiny.

# #Gutcheck

<140: Intuition is the first sign, everything else is simply confirmation.

(67 characters)

# #Gutcheck

**P**eople say that the first sign you get is your intuition. You'll find yourself in lots of situations in life and sometimes the only thing you can turn to is your gut. You don't need the negative situation to hit you in the face; all you need to rely on is that feeling of uneasiness, unyielding doubt, and uncertainty. If the situation doesn't feel right, more than likely it's not. It's like meeting that person whose energy just feels bad and later on you learn that they are bad. It's just that simple. Learn to trust your gut in your personal and professional life, it usually never fails you.

**AFFIRMATION:** I receive the discerning power that I possess. My discernment protects me from things that are not aligned with my purpose.

# #OutTheBoxStateOfMind

< 140: The comfort zone is a dead zone that will never get into the end zone.

(55 characters)

# #OutTheBoxStateOfMind

The comfort zone is defined as a behavioral state where a person operates in a sense without risk. Most of the time people are scared of what others may think when they do something out of the "norm." You're afraid that your friends, family, or co-workers may not accept that you've gone against the grain. You can't let life box you in when you are seeking greatness; when you're on the quest to do more than the ordinary. Challenge yourself to do something different, something that makes you feel like you're operating on the edge of insanity. A box has limitations. Those same limits will become the things that perpetuate mediocrity in your life. The only person stopping you from great heights is you. Step outside of the walls of the ordinary and achieve a life that is fit for only the regal.

**AFFIRMATION:** Life is what I make it and a box cannot bring me full circle. I will not limit my success. I will always live life outside of the box.

# #ChampionIT

< 140: Survival isn't just about being fit; it's about being smart.

(60 characters)

# #ChampionIT

**M**y mom always told me, "Whatever doesn't kill you can only make you better." I think this has been some of the hardest advice to embrace. Life comes with so much adversity. It's just the reality of living. You will have heartache, loss, betrayal; the list goes on and on. What you have to remember about your journey is that these unpredictable, emotionally time consuming, and hurtful situations are designed to make you smarter. Now you may be saying, I thought the old saying was it makes you better, not smarter? That is true, but the flaw in stronger is that even if you continue to grow stronger, the strength is useless if you don't have the understanding of how to utilize that strength. You have to learn from the negative situation to grow in your greatness. A survivor's testimony has the most impact because they not only lived to tell their story but they are smart enough to tell their story.

**AFFIRMATION:** I am better not because I survived it but because I championed it.

# #Learn2Listen

<140: In order to be better, we must listen to understand, never simply to respond.

(63 characters)

# #Learn2Listen

**L**earning to be quiet may be one of the toughest parts of being human. Truly, most people don't listen for understanding, they listen to respond. That's why most communication fails; however, to learn we must become greater listeners. It's like learning the lyrics to a new song, before you can sing the song and feel the message you must first, shut up and listen. In life, we must take the time to listen to those around us so we can learn more about ourselves.

**AFFIRMATION:** I am so much better because I take the time not only to hear those around me but to listen to their messages bestowed upon me.

# #AWorkInProgress

<140: Learn to grow with your goals because if you're not growing then you might as well be dead. (91 characters)

# #AWorkInProgress

**W**hen you are trying to reach a goal, you have to be flexible. You have to understand that growth is a key concept of living. Your hair grows, your nails grow, and plants grow, so why shouldn't you grow as your goals grow? Take time to find out who you are and what you believe in. As you grow, your goals and your vision will evolve. You may learn that the person you were yesterday is no longer aligned with the goal that you have for today or tomorrow. Accept that change is necessary in fulfilling your purpose. While you're chasing your dreams, take some time to look in the mirror and appreciate the changes that are happening inside of you. With every laugh line, every friend lost, every love forgotten, you are one step closer to the goal that is to be attained. Embrace it, love it and own your progress.

**AFFIRMATION:** I embrace that every day, I have the right to grow. I love the changes that I see happening within me. Change is good as I work towards my life's aspirations.

# #ForgivenessIsFreedom

<140: A heart that forgives is free from the pain of the past.

(56 characters)

# #ForgivenessIsFreedom

Life comes with so many ups and downs that if you live long enough, most of the people who have offended you, you won't even remember.  Learning to forgive those who hurt you, frees up space in your life. The freedom of forgiveness gives you room to live a life that's full, fun, and free.  Remembering that life is too short to carry around the pain of the past is even more reason to embrace the power of forgiveness.

**AFFIRMATION:** I forgive those who hurt me. I receive that freedom that comes along with forgiveness.  I am now free.

# #IsWhatItIs

< 140: Make peace with what is b/c it will be, what it is, no matter your response.

(76 characters)

# #IsWhatItIs

**A**ccept what is beyond your control. A good friend always told me, "It's going to be what it is." I used to get so upset when others didn't meet my expectations or when a temporary situation became an inconvenience. I had to learn that this statement wasn't about complacency but about a peace-of-mind. Letting things be what they are allows you to understand the human nature of people and the unpredictability of situations. It gives you the freedom to live life fully because you've accepted the variety of each day. It also relieves you of unrealistic accountability for circumstances that are not your responsibility. When you learn to adjust and adapt to what life throws your way, you'll end up on the starting lineup and maybe even being named the MVP. Make the most of it all. Don't dwell on what is not, focus on what is. Remember that you have the ability to mold *what is* in the image of what you need it to be. No one controls the situation unto which they are born, but what they can control is the life that they live.

**AFFIRMATION:** I embrace the things that are within my grasp and those that are out of my reach. No matter what is, I understand that my life is what I make of it.

# The *PASSION* Affirmations

# #GetYourCrew

< 140: Real friendships don't come easily so when you find them, keep them.

(68 characters)

# #GetYourCrew

**F**inding "real" friends doesn't have to be a process. It's something that can come naturally. Everybody that likes the same designer labels as you don't translate into your new BFF (best friend for life). Choose your friends carefully. Ultimately, they are a reflection of you.  Does he/she have the same life goals? Does this person have a moral compass that is aligned with where you're going? Is this someone that you don't mind people saying your name and his/hers in the same sentence? Does this person respect the other important people in your life? If your answer is yes, this just may be your crew.

**AFFIRMATION:** My friends are a reflection of me. They complement me and I, in turn, complement them.

# #DevelopYourGreatness

< 140: Good things come to those who work, so keep putting in that work.

(65 characters)

# #DevelopYourGreatness

Growing up in the inner city can be rough. Growing up in the suburbs has its challenges too. There are always opportunities to make excuses or get down on yourself because of your situation. We complain about what we don't have and then make case for how what we do have, could be better. The reality is, you have to make the best of what you have. It doesn't matter if your parents divorced or you never knew your mom, that's your best hand and you have to shuffle the cards until you get a win. From the outside, people don't care about your circumstances, they just want results. Be the best you that you can be. All life wants to know is...are you great enough? If you want to be anything in life, the journey starts with right now, not yesterday. Don't sit around waiting for your talent to get better, make moves to study and master your craft.

**AFFIRMATION:** I'm better than just good. I am great. I have greatness in me and I will take steps every day to be that much greater.

# #ConsistencyIsKey

<140: Where there is no consistency there is a lack of commitment.

(50 characters)

# #ConsistencyIsKey

I'm sure you've heard the expression "it might not happen when you want it to happen." True. I am a witness to the fact that it more than likely will NOT happen when YOU want it to happen. Does that mean you give up? Does that mean you quit? NO! You have to continually remind yourself of this on your journey to reaching personal and professional prosperity. You have to commit to doing it over and over and over and over again. You have to do it until not only you believe but others do as well. I once interviewed a running back for the Baltimore Ravens and when I asked him how he made it to the NFL he reminded me that "consistency is key." Consistency is key in building trust and strong relationships. Consistency is key in mastering your craft. Consistency is even key in managing your finances and growing wealth. Those who "make it" in life do so because they never stopped, they were always consistent and people saw their commitment.

**AFFIRMATION:** I'll happily do what I am called to do as much as it needs to be done. My consistency is a reflection of my commitment to the work I've been created to do.

# #MakeItHappen

< 140: Get yours because there's enough for all of us.

(47 characters)

# #MakeItHappen

**O**ne of the greatest advertising campaigns in American history was Nike's "Just Do It" campaign. Sometimes, you have to apply the obvious to life and just do it. Don't question who or what it will take to get it done, just focus on making it happen. Step out on faith. Steer clear of those who will distract you. People will always be strategically placed in your life to try to deter you from what you're called to do. Use all of your talents, resources and strength to make it happen. If getting into the studio is what you feel in your heart, you should be doing what you need to do to find an engineer. Googling, cold calling, showing up, are all things necessary to get you one step closer to making your first single. It doesn't matter what comes of the single, what matters is that you'll never have to operate in the state of, "what if I made it happen?" No one has ever achieved their dream without making it happen.

**AFFIRMATION:** I am a doer and not a dreamer. I will make my goals happen because my goals are my dreams with deadlines.

# #FaceITWithFlare

< 140: You have to face it to make it.

(31 characters)

# #FaceITWithFlare

**D**welling on the unknown leads to years of complacency. If God wanted you to know exactly what HE had in store for you then HE wouldn't put you through a series of tests. Think about how life was as a student. I recall the number of days that I got up in the morning, got dressed, went to school, learned new things, took notes, and went home to study what I learned. When the next day came around I didn't know what challenges I would face walking out of my front door. I didn't know if someone would try to do harm to me, if I would be the victim of one of Baltimore's many crimes. I had no idea. What I did know was that I wanted my diploma, and although my home wasn't in the best neighborhood, and although my school wasn't in the best neighborhood, I didn't let that deter me from getting what I wanted.

Yes, I experienced some failures. There were some classes that I didn't do as well in as others. There were some relationships that I could have nurtured a little better. There were some loved ones that I lost during these years. But I didn't let it stop me from getting my diploma. You may even experience failure after failure, making you believe that "it" is impossible. Facing it is not at all about the situation, but everything about your response to it. So take it on and face it with flare! Be fearless and flattering in all that you do. Make people know that your situation does not determine your outcome. Be victorious as you walk life's journey. Always remember to keep your head up, shoulders back and a smile on your face. Your "flare", or positive response to the situation, will always keep the outcome in your favor.

**AFFIRMATION:** I am facing every one of life's obstacles with charisma and dignity. This situation will not change the person I am.

# #PeopleWannaKnowMe

< 140: Be the one in the room that everyone wants to know.

(51 characters)

# #PeopleWannaKnowMe

**S**tart harvesting your greatness and become that person that everyone wants to know. You do your thing with efficiency and swag. Don't only execute the task, but do it with your own signature style. Become the person that walks in the room and commands the attention of everyone. Speak to everyone from the doorman to the senior level executives and have them call you by name. Make a conscious effort to make a positive impression. Acknowledge those who society has kicked to the curb; your smile or hello could change that person's day. When people want to know you, opportunities will always come your way. .

**AFFIRMATION:** I am the one that everyone wants to know.

# #InITNotOfIT

<140: Just because you're in it doesn't mean you have to become it.

(61 characters)

# #InITNotOfIT

**E**very situation in life is not going to be sweet. Every experience is not going to have your desired outcome. Every person you encounter is not going to have your best interest at heart. However, you don't have to conform to what's happening around you. You don't have to become negative because you are surrounded by negativity. You don't have to become hopeless, when the situation looks bleak. You don't have to be vengeful when someone treats you poorly. Real life scenarios reveal the true character of a person. This doesn't mean that taking the high road comes easily or at first attempt. What it does mean is that you have the ability to control how you respond to life's scenarios.

**AFFIRMATION:** I give up the desire to control situations and I embrace my power to claim only positive outcomes.

# #NoBlurredLines

<140: Boundaries are the lines that distinguish the mediocre from the great.

(70 characters)

# #NoBlurredLines

How low can you go? No...I'm not talking about limbo! How much are you willing to compromise just to fit in or have a temporary sense of satisfaction? Many people lower their standards to get something that they think that they want and not what is truly created for them. If you have to lower your standards for it, you may need to ask yourself, is this aligned with where I am going in life? Don't allow someone or something to compromise who you are. Ask yourself, "What do I deserve? Where am I going? Who or what do I see for my future?" Then write your responses down and never stray from them. It's easy to conform to what everyone else is doing, but when you are seeking something extraordinary you have to go against the grain. The great ones always break the mold. The question is, are you willing to set and maintain boundaries necessary for success? If you find yourself always having to lower your standards, reassess your goals. You may be trying to grow in a direction that is not aligned with who you are destined to be.

**AFFIRMATION:** It's okay for me to know what I want and how I want it. I am excited about the standards I have set and I will keep them close to my heart.

# #NoNegativity

<140: All business isn't good business, so don't accept every job that comes your way.

(80 characters)

# #NoNegativity

It's painful loving people who really don't love themselves. That's a gem that I got from my dad. If you're the optimistic type, you'll always see the good in people—something my best friend says is an admirable yet epic flaw that she sees in me. When you are looking at the best, it's sometimes hard to see that it wasn't right from the start. Work on seeing things for what they are and not what you want them to be, then start building from there. Also, acknowledge that some people are simply toxic. Avoid these situations at all costs. This doesn't mean that you won't experience situations in life that have an unforeseen or unfavorable outcomes but the overall experience will leave a positive imprint on your life. Don't hesitate to say no, when you know, it's simply not right.

**AFFIRMATION:** I only claim positive situations and results from the start. I am okay with saying no to negativity.

# #HiHater

< 140: Envy is a form a flattery, so let the haters hate.

(50 Characters)

# #HiHater

**N**ow, if you're not hip to the game, you may want to do some research on this one. What I mean by "shaking those haters off" is recognize when someone doesn't admire you, they envy you. Notice how every time something bad happens in your life, they're quick to put your business on "News at 11". This is the same person that when you achieve something great, you see that hate in that person's eyes. He or she is so jealous of you and your swag that he/she can barely get through the day. This is a person that is consumed with envy. Identify the hater and shake him/her off; that person is not your friend. This person is waiting to expose your deepest secrets; simply to take the focus off of his/her lack and shortcomings. Shake him/her off and get a true friend.

**AFFIRMATION:** I embrace those who challenge me, they were created to help me become a better me.

# The *PROSPERITY* Affirmations

# #EmbraceTheNow

<140: Decide to never approach life with foggy lenses that way you'll always see the sunshine.

(88 characters)

# #EmbraceTheNow

**N**ever resent the moment. I struggled with this most of my journey. Some days it would get so tough for me not to be angered by things that were happening in my life that I found myself developing a spirit of bitterness and resentment. I couldn't understand why I was not in love, or why he dumped me or why my salary didn't reflect my effort. I later began to see that it wasn't about the situation, but my response to it. I saw myself missing out on the joys of today because my lenses were foggy. Resentment takes energy and consumes lots of positive mental space. Your current situation is not created to make you angry; it is created to perfect you. It's designed to make you better, to make you wiser so that others can benefit from your story. Life is a combination of choices and experiences that shape who you are. Inevitably, you chose the space that you live in mentally. Always approach life with the goal of happiness in mind.

**AFFIRMATION:** Today I chose to be happy no matter my current situation. My situation today is just to reveal a better me tomorrow.

# #ByeFelicia

< 140: Sometimes you have to walk away to walk into your destiny.

(58 characters)

# #ByeFelicia

**Y**ou meet someone that you think you want to grow old with (or at least go on a 3rd date with) and then you realize your visions aren't aligned. Your perspectives are contradictory and your signals are crossed. The simple realization is, you just may not be ready for this kind of endeavor. Sometimes you have to embrace the simple realities of they may cost you your sanity or even your future. It's not worth your destiny to compromise your integrity. Straighten up and learn to play by your instincts. You may have to leave the party, hang up the phone, or give back the keys to reclaim your destiny. Saying good bye isn't always that bad, especially when it prepares you for the right opportunity.

**AFFIRMATION:** I'm okay with saying "no." I am too valuable to compromise my mind, body and or spirit. I am worth more than a compromise.

# #GetInvolved

<140: We are created to serve.

(24 characters)

# #GetInvolved

**Y**our talents were given to you so that you can help others?  You were given special gifts because you were created to be of service.  This has been coined as *servant leadership*. Commit to a cause and take action. There are people that need your gift to accomplish something positive. Every step you take, big or small, builds towards a much greater goal.  Always remember, you are blessed to be a blessing to others.

**AFFIRMATION:** I will use my unique gifts to positively impact the world. I am a servant leader.

# #DoITWithASmile

<140: Smiling makes the journey sweet.

(32 characters)

# #DoITWithASmile

**M**y big brother always told me you catch more bees with honey than vinegar. It took some time for this quote to make sense in my head, but then it clicked. In order to taste the sweetness of life, you have to put a little honey on it. Make it sweet and do it with a smile. A smile opens up your heart to positive emotions and it gives people around you a sense of warmth.  No matter what journey you are taking in life, don't do it begrudgingly, do it with a smile.

**AFFIRMATION:** My smile may be the only sunshine in someone's day.  I embrace being a source of light.

# #BeGood2You

<140: Teach people how to treat you by first being good to yourself.

(62 characters)

# #BeGood2You

**W**e seek love, confirmation, and validation from everyone else but ourselves. We spend most of our minutes, hours, days, months and years working to please others. We often forget ourselves during the process. Take the time to reflect on all the good you do in the world and remember to always be good to you.

**AFFIRMATION:** I will treat myself good until the end of time. I embrace the possibilities of being good to me.

# #Follow1Course

< 140: Follow one course until successful.

(35 characters)

# #Follow1Course

**F**OCUS, FOCUS, FOCUS! You can't go both ways down a one way street. You can't be double-minded and extraordinary at the same. You have to choose a path and explore the infinite possibilities along that road. Develop a focus in your life and work until you become successful. Apply focus in your personal, professional, spiritual and physical life. Success in life starts with simply making a choice to focus.

**AFFIRMATION:** I have chosen the path to my success. I will stick to it until success is achieved.

# #BeEXTRA!

< 140: Embrace the power to create a life that is better than the ordinary.

(68 characters)

# #BeEXTRA!

**E**xtraordinary people make extraordinary sacrifices in order to live an extraordinary life. BE the change that you'd like to see. BE the hope that you want to embrace. BE the inspiration that you feel society is lacking. BE the example of love that the world lacks. BE compassionate, BE loving, BE empowered and more importantly BE EXTRAORDINARY.

**AFFIRMATION:** I was created to be more than the ordinary. I am EXTRAORDINARY.

# EXTRAORDINARY QUOTES

# *EXTRAORDINARY QUOTES*

**H**ave you ever talked to someone and that one thing they said left you speechless?   During my time as a journalist, I've had the opportunity to meet and interview lots of amazing people doing more than the ordinary.  Each of these people left me with jewels that are with me to this day.  Here, I encourage you to read each quote, sit and think about how it can be applied to your life and journal your way to purpose, passion and prosperity.

# "We are blessed to be a blessing."

**~Nick Cannon**, *Actor, Host, Executive Producer, Philanthropist*

*How can you be a blessing to others?*

_____

_____

_____

_____

_____

_____

_____

_____

_____

_____

_____

_____

_____

_____

_____

_____

_____

# "FOCUS on your position and not your condition."

**~Chuck Pagano**, *Head Coach for Indianapolis Colts*

*What areas of your life do you need to change your focus? Why?*

_____

_____

_____

_____

_____

_____

_____

_____

_____

_____

_____

_____

_____

_____

_____

_____

_____

# "Consistency is Key"

**~Ray Lewis**, *Former Super Bowl MVP, Sports Announcer*

*Where in your life do you need to be more consistent? How will consistency lead to a prosperous life full of passion and purpose?*

_____

_____

_____

_____

_____

_____

_____

_____

_____

_____

_____

_____

_____

_____

_____

# "Follow your EFFORT!"

**~Mark Cuban**, *Owner, Dallas Mavericks*

*What do your present day efforts say about where you are going? What areas should you center your effort?*

_____

_____

_____

_____

_____

_____

_____

_____

_____

_____

_____

_____

_____

_____

_____

_____

# "You can't compromise your Christian principles."

**~Tony Dungy**, *First African American Head Coach to win a Super Bowl*

*When have you compromised who you are or what you want? What was the outcome? What areas of your life should you never compromise?*

_____

_____

_____

_____

_____

_____

_____

_____

_____

_____

_____

_____

_____

_____

# "Get your priorities in order!"

**~Bobby Bowden**, *Legendary Head Coach for the Florida State Gators*

*List your priorities below. Are these priorities aligned with the purpose you'd like to fulfill?*

_____

_____

_____

_____

_____

_____

_____

_____

_____

_____

_____

_____

_____

_____

_____

_____

_____

_____

# "Music empowered me to be okay with who I am and what I wanted to be in life."

**~Clinton Sparks**, *DJ & Producer for Beyonce', Lady Gaga, Pit Bull, Akon*

*What empowers you? How can what empowers you become a part of your purpose?*

_____

_____

_____

_____

_____

_____

_____

_____

_____

_____

_____

_____

_____

_____

# "I like keeping life as normal as possible."

**~Joan Lunden**, *Award-winning journalist, cancer survivor, motivational speaker*

*Who or what keeps you grounded? How or why?*

_____

_____

_____

_____

_____

_____

_____

_____

_____

_____

_____

_____

_____

_____

_____

# "FOCUS!
# You have to be focused on the task at hand and focused on what you want to achieve and the goal you want to accomplish."

**~Russell Westbrook,**
*Point Guard, Oklahoma City Thunder, MVP of the 64th Annual NBA All Star Game*

*What is the goal you want to accomplish? How can you focus more on achieving this goal?*

_____

_____

_____

_____

_____

_____

_____

_____

_____

_____

_____

# "A proper legacy can't be left in a will…a proper legacy can be left in full to everyone because it's what you give of yourself."

**~Coach Bill Courtney**, *Academy Award Winning Coach, Entrepreneur and Author of "Against the Grain"*

*What mark do you want to leave on the world? How?*

_____

_____

_____

_____

_____

_____

_____

_____

_____

_____

_____

_____

# EXTRAORDINARY TIPS

## TIPS TO IDENTIFYING PURPOSE

» Keep a purpose journal. Write down the things you enjoy spending time doing.

» Question yourself. What is your "difference that will make a difference"?

» List your interests and passions. What motivates and energizes you?

» Write down what you love. Focus on things that you love rather than looking at reason.

» Find your joy. What things make me feel happy?

» Use backwards planning. What would your Purposeful Life look like at 20, 30, 40, 50 or even 60 years old?

## TIPS TO BEING PASSIONATE

- » Respect that life is a process.
- » Never over complicate life by putting the idea of perfection on yourself or others.
- » Don't carry the weight of not expressing your feelings.
- » Don't allow a lack of trust to impact your happiness.
- » Take emotional risks.
- » Acknowledge your successes, big and small.
- » Make peace with your past.
- » Figure out what makes you happy and seek it out until you find it.

## TIPS TO RECEIVING PROSPERITY

- » Be Open.
- » Be Patient.
- » Be Understanding.
- » Be Faithful
- » Be Humble.
- » Be Thankful
- » Be Extraordinary

# EXTRAORDINARY PRAYERS

## POWERFUL Prayers

My early thirties proved to be quite challenging. Most days I was alone, without family or friends in a strange city full of even stranger people and unknown opportunities. Instead of looking outside for conversation, insight and guidance, I would sit in my one bedroom apartment and simply talk to the Lord. During that silent season, I committed myself to writing a few prayers that I am now sharing with you. I wrote these prayers on index cards, kept them close to my heart (in my purse to be exact) and pulled them out whenever I needed to hear from the Lord. I hope these prayers bless you as much as they have blessed me.

## *Spiritual Growth*

Dear God, I pray in this season that I grow tremendously as a Christian through the study of your word. I pray that reading your word allows me to grow closer to you, so that I feel not only that you are my father, but that you are also my friend. Lord, I thank you for your word and the wisdom that comes off of the pages of the Bible that helps me reflect on my ways. During that reflection, I pray that it is made clear to me if my ways and actions are aligned with YOU and Your will. AMEN

## *Spiritual Growth*

GOD, I ask that you grant me the wisdom to seek your word to battle any struggles in my life. I pray that my study of your word helps me spread your gospel eagerly and efficiently. I thank you for this time of growth. I thank you for sharing your miracles with me and the world. Only you can create a word that is everlasting. I am thankful that you are giving me a chance to know and love you through your word. AMEN

## *Speaking Life*

Lord, please let your Holy Spirit come over me so much so that, I only speak life; for words have life. I pray that you give me the foresight to speak things that only build others up, not break them down. I pray that you use me as a vessel when I speak to and encounter those who don't know You. Dear God, I pray that the meditations of my heart are aligned with your will. I pray that everything I speak gives you all of the honor, the glory, and the praise. AMEN

## *Assignment*

Dear God, Jesus Christ. I seek your supernatural favor to  eloquently, efficiently, and extraordinarily live out your assignment for my life in such I want to live in a way that people are so taken by my gifts that all they can assume is that my gifts come from You. I pray that I seek your faith and your face in all that I do.  Dear Lord, I ask that the Holy Spirit shines in every area of my life—from the cubicle, to the conference room and any other place that I go on your behalf.  AMEN

## *Assignment*

Dear Lord, I pray that the Holy Spirit moves on the decision makers. I am aware that the assignment you have for my life is great. I ask that you protect my walk, my heart, my family and my overall being while I do your will. I pray for your continued supernatural presence as I live out the vision you have created in me. AMEN

## *Faith*

Jesus, I pray for supernatural and unyielding faith that the vision you have planted in me since I was _____ years old _____ _____ is real and that you are working every day for it to come to pass. I pray that I recognize that this vision is not about me, but only for your glory. I pray in expectation that you will strategically place me in a professional capacity that will only allow you to be glorified. I pray that you continue to guard my heart, my mind, my finances, my soul, and my physical well-being during and until my dreams come to pass.

## *Faith*

Dear God, I pray that you continue to supernaturally open doors that the average person cannot even fathom. I thank you Lord for your angels here on earth, that remind me that you are real. I thank you for this and all things. I thank you for every moment, past and present, that keep me moving forward in expectation of your will. AMEN

## Patience

Dear Lord, I pray for your power. I pray for your peace. I pray for your patience while I am awaiting your promises. Lord, I pray for the judgment to call on you when I am irritated, frustrated and discouraged thinking that your promises are not real. I pray that you continue to strategically place me in situations that test my faith; situations that mold my spirit, so that I can grow more patient in all my ways. Lord, thank you for blessing me with your peace that soothes my soul as your will for my life is done in your time. Lord, I thank you for allowing me to be mature enough to see that I will receive your blessings when you know I am prepared enough to receive them in all fullness. AMEN

## *Patience (mate)*

Jesus, I pray for an unyielding patience while I wait on the things that you have for my life. I pray for a mate that is a provider and a leader; someone who will love you first and that is willing to submit to your will. I pray for a man who will treat me like a precious gem; someone who will value, support and embrace my love and loyalty forever. I pray for a man who wants to start and build a life with me and that will treat me as his complement. I pray for the patience to wait on a man who's just as excited to show me off as he is to spend intimate time. I pray for the gift of discernment while I am waiting patiently on the man that you have for me. I pray that you remove any spirit of loneliness within me while I wait on the man that has been created to make me a better woman of God. AMEN

## Deliverance

God, I seek your strength and deliverance from any demonic spirit of depression or doubt in my life. After every failure and disappointment, please shield me from low self-esteem, sadness, and depression. I ask that you come into my heart and allow the Holy Spirit to make me feel full and loved when I feel lonely. Remind me that you are my closest friend at my lowest points. I seek only positive thoughts and feelings about my value, my worth and my abilities. Help me to see that only greatness resides in me. AMEN

## *Deliverance*

Lord, I ask for the power to accept the things about me that I cannot change. I ask for your healing grace over the losses in my life. I ask for forgiveness over the decisions that I regret. I pray that you deliver my soul from feelings of loss, abandonment, and bitterness. I pray that I can make strides towards happiness and wholeness of life, every single day of my life. I pray for deliverance from any spirit that is not of your will. AMEN

## *Accountability*

Dear Lord, I ask that you make me accountable for my actions. I pray that I seek your will in all that I do. I pray that I can accept the criticisms of my flaws and that I can be humble enough in knowing that I am not perfect. I seek guidance from you Lord that I do not stray away from being a better me. I seek your face in working through my flaws and in taking responsibility for who I am. I pray that your spirit continues to humble me as I grow to be a living example of your will and your ways. AMEN

## Completion

God, I pray that you remove the spirit of fear and insecurity from my heart and my mind. I pray that I complete the tasks that you have assigned to me. I release all procrastination, fear and doubt because I know that those are not spirits of your perfect will. I pray for the ability to recognize when I am putting things off and then ask for the strength to complete the task at hand. I pray that I do this with no hesitation and or self-doubt. AMEN

## Completion

Dear God, I pray that the spirits of fear and doubt come out of me in your name. I pray that the issues that reside in me never keep me from doing the work that needs to be done. Please remove anything from my life that keeps me stagnate. I seek your presence so that I never have an excuse to not complete what needs to be done. I pray that in doing all these things, you make me know that I am competent and capable to complete anything that you've asked me to do. AMEN

# *Thanksgiving*

Lord, I thank you for my life. I thank you for every good and bad thing that has happened that has molded me into the person I am today. I thank you for every new day that I can experience your light. I seek a spirit that is so thankful that I cry out to you with praise. I thank you Lord for loving me, even when I didn't love myself. AMEN

# EXTRAORDINARY
# WORD OF GOD

# USE THE WORD TO BECOME WISE

There were many days where I don't know what I would have done if it wasn't for the comfort and guidance that I found in the word of the Lord. I literally cut out hearts and wrote scriptures on them and placed them all around my desk at work. It is important to ingest and digest the word, daily, in times of despair and in times of hope. I wanted to share with you areas of my life where scriptures from the Bible guided my heart and, better yet, my response. Write them on a sticky note, dress your posted goals with scripture, but more importantly, keep these words in your heart. I encourage you to stand on God's word when you are on your journey of becoming the most Extraordinary YOU that you can be.

Now you may ask, how do I "stand" on God's word? Here are my suggestions:

- Commit to reading God's word every day, even if it's just for five (5) minutes. The amount of time it takes you to go to the refrigerator and pour a glass of water is the same amount of time it takes to acquire daily inspiration. Commit to reading His word. <-I promise it will be more refreshing than that glass of water.

- Memorize a few scriptures that truly speak to the heart and soul of the person you strive to be.

- Purchase a devotional and really allow yourself time to grow in the word of the Lord.

- Take notes in church or when you watch sermons.

- Connect with a body of believers who will remind you of God's grace, His glory and principles on a regular basis.

- Listen and ask questions. Admitting that you don't understand something shows humility and a desire to learn and better yourself.

*Adversity*

"If God be for us, who can be against us?" *~Romans 8:31*

"Consider it all joy, my brethren, when you encounter various trials, knowing that the testing of your faith produces endurance. And let endurance have its perfect result, so that you may be perfect and complete, lacking in nothing." *~ James 1:2-4*

"A friend loves at all times and a brother is born for adversity." *~ Proverbs 17:17*

"And we know that God causes all things to work together for good to those who love God, to those who are called according to His purpose." *~ Romans 8:28*

"Do not fear, for I am with you; do not anxiously look about you, for I am your God I will strengthen you, surely I will help you, surely I will uphold you with My righteous right hand." *~ Isaiah 41:10*

"Cast your burden upon the LORD and He will sustain you; He will never allow the righteous to be shaken." *~ Psalms 55:22*

"These things I have spoken to you, so that in Me you may have peace In the world you have tribulation, but take courage; I have overcome the world." *~ John 16:33*

"Yet those who wait for the LORD Will gain new strength; they will mount up with wings like eagles, They will run and not get tired, They will walk and not become weary." *~ Isaiah 40:31*

# Attitude

"Then your heart will become proud and you will forget the LORD your God who brought you out from the land of Egypt, out of the house of slavery." *~ Deuteronomy 8:14*

"I will also break down your pride of power; I will also make your sky like iron and your earth like bronze." *~ Leviticus 26:19*

"He has done mighty deeds with His arm; He has scattered those who were proud in the thoughts of their heart." *~ Luke 1:51*

"God is opposed to the proud, but gives grace to the humble." *~ James 4:6*

"Though He scoffs at the scoffers, yet He gives grace to the afflicted." *~ Proverbs 3:34*

"Charm is deceitful and beauty is vain, But a woman who fears the LORD, she shall be praised." *~ Proverbs 31:30*

"As a ring of gold in a swine's snout; so is a beautiful woman who lacks discretion." *~ Proverbs 11:22*

"Do not desire her beauty in your heart, nor let her capture you with her eyelids." *~ Proverbs 6:25*

# Belief

"A double-minded man is unstable in all his ways."
*~James 1:8*

"One Lord, one faith, one baptism." *~ Ephesians 4:5*

"To Timothy, my true child in the faith: Grace, mercy and peace from God the Father and Christ Jesus our Lord." *~1 Timothy 1:2*

"All who are with me greet you Greet those who love us in the faith Grace be with you all." *~ Titus 3:15*

Jesus said to him, "I am the way, and the truth, and the life; no one comes to the Father but through Me." *~ John 14:6*

"I am amazed that you are so quickly deserting Him who called you by the grace of Christ, for a different gospel; which is really not another; only there are some who are disturbing you and want to distort the gospel of Christ. But even if we, or an angel from heaven, should preach to you a gospel contrary to what we have preached to you, he is to be accursed!" *~ Galatians 1:6-9*

"Retain the standard of sound words which you have heard from me, in the faith and love which are in Christ Jesus. Guard, through the Holy Spirit who dwells in us, the treasure which has been entrusted to you." *~2 Timothy 1:13-14*

# Closure

"The law of the Lord is perfect, reviving the soul; the testimony of the Lord is sure, making wise the simple." *~Psalm 19:7*

"All Scripture is breathed out by God and profitable for teaching, for reproof, for correction, and for training in righteousness." *~2 Timothy 3:16*

"Paul, a servant of Christ Jesus, called to be an apostle, set apart for the gospel of God, which he promised beforehand through his prophets in the holy Scriptures, concerning his Son, who was descended from David according to the flesh and was declared to be the Son of God in power according to the Spirit of holiness by his resurrection from the dead, Jesus Christ our Lord, through whom we have received grace and apostleship to bring about the obedience of faith for the sake of his name among all the nations..." *~Romans 1:1-32*

"When Jesus had received the sour wine, he said, "It is finished," and he bowed his head and gave up his spirit." *~John 19:30*

"For God so loved the world, that he gave his only Son, that whoever believes in him should not perish but have eternal life. For God did not send his Son into the world to condemn the world, but in order that the world might be saved through him." *~John 3:16-17*

"But he answered, 'It is written, man shall not live by bread alone, but by every word that comes from the mouth of God'." *~Matthew 4:4*

"Heaven and earth will pass away, but my words will not pass away." *~ Luke 21:33*

"Heaven and earth will pass away, but my words will not pass away." *~ Matthew 24:35*

"For truly, I say to you, until heaven and earth pass away, not an iota, not a dot, will pass from the Law until all is accomplished." *~Matthew 5:18*

"For God so loved the world, that he gave his only Son, that whoever believes in him should not perish but have eternal life." *~John 3:16*

# Completion

"The Lord will fulfill his purpose for me; your steadfast love, O Lord, endures forever. Do not forsake the work of your hands." *~Psalm 138:8*

"These things I have spoken to you while I am still with you. But the Helper, the Holy Spirit, whom the Father will send in my name, he will teach you all things and bring to your remembrance all that I have said to you. Peace I leave with you; my peace I give to you. Not as the world gives do I give to you. Let not your hearts be troubled, neither let them be afraid." *~John 14:25-27*

"For those whom he foreknew he also predestined to be conformed to the image of his Son, in order that he might be the firstborn among many brothers." *~Romans 8:29*

"But do not overlook this one fact, beloved, that with the Lord one day is as a thousand years, and a thousand years as one day." *~2 Peter 3:8*

"Behold! I tell you a mystery. We shall not all sleep, but we shall all be changed, in a moment, in the twinkling of an eye, at the last trumpet. For the trumpet will sound, and the dead will be raised imperishable, and we shall be changed. For this perishable body must put on the imperishable, and this mortal body must put on immortality. When the perishable puts on the imperishable, and the mortal puts on immortality, then shall come to pass

the saying that is written: "Death is swallowed up in victory." "O death, where is your victory? O death, where is your sting?"*~ 1 Corinthians 15:51-55*

"But when the perfect comes, the partial will pass away." *~1 Corinthians 13:10*

# Doubt

"I can do all things, through Christ who strengthens me." *~ Philippians 4:13*

"These things I have written to you who believe in the name of the Son of God, so that you may know that you have eternal life." *~1 John 5:13*

"Sustain me according to Your word, that I may live; And do not let me be ashamed of my hope." *~ Psalms 119:116*

"Behold, I am with you and will keep you wherever you go, and will bring you back to this land; for I will not leave you until I have done what I have promised you." *~ Genesis 28:15*

"But these have been written so that you may believe that Jesus is the Christ, the Son of God; and that believing you may have life in His name. *~ John 20:31*

"And He said, 'Certainly I will be with you, and this shall be the sign to you that it is I who have sent you: when you have brought the people out of Egypt, you shall worship God at this mountain'." *~ Exodus 3:12*

*Empathy*

"Be kind to one another, tenderhearted, forgiving one another, as God in Christ forgave you."
*~Ephesians 4:32*

"Rejoice with those who rejoice, weep with those who weep." *~Romans 12:15*

"So whatever you wish that others would do to you, do also to them, for this is the Law and the Prophets." *~Matthew 7:12*

"This is my commandment, that you love one another as I have loved you." *~John 15:12*

"Let no corrupting talk come out of your mouths, but only such as is good for building up, as fits the occasion, that it may give grace to those who hear."
*~Ephesians 4:29*

"Finally, all of you, have unity of mind, sympathy, brotherly love, a tender heart, and a humble mind."
*~1 Peter 3:8*

"Do nothing from rivalry or conceit, but in humility count others more significant than yourselves."
*~Philippians 2:3*

"Put on then, as God's chosen ones, holy and beloved, compassionate hearts, kindness, humility, meekness, and patience. "*~Colossians 3:12*

# Empire

"From the wilderness and this Lebanon, even as far as the great river, the river Euphrates, all the land of the Hittites, and as far as the Great Sea toward the setting of the sun will be your territory." ~ *Joshua 1:*

Then he charged them and said to them, "I am about to be gathered to my people; bury me with my fathers in the cave that is in the field of Ephron the Hittite, in the cave that is in the field of Machpelah, which is before Mamre, in the land of Canaan, which Abraham bought along with the field from Ephron the Hittite for a burial site." ~ *Genesis 49:29-30*

"For his sons carried him to the land of Canaan and buried him in the cave of the field of Machpelah before Mamre, which Abraham had bought along with the field for a burial site from Ephron the Hittite." ~ *Genesis 50:13*

"So David sent and inquired about the woman. And one said, "Is this not Bathsheba, the daughter of Eliam, the wife of Uriah the Hittite?" David sent messengers and took her, and when she came to him, he lay with her; and when she had purified herself from her uncleanness, she returned to her house. The woman conceived; and she sent and told David, and said, "I am pregnant." ~*2 Samuel 11:3-24*

"Now there was a famine in the land; so Abram went down to Egypt to sojourn there, for the famine was severe in the land. " ~ *Genesis 12:10*

"The one who conquers will have this heritage, and I will be his God and he will be my son. But as for the cowardly, the faithless, the detestable, as for murderers, the sexually immoral, sorcerers, idolaters, and all liars, their portion will be in the lake that burns with fire and sulfur, which is the second death."~ *Revelation 21:7-8*

"Therefore I tell you, whatever you ask for in prayer, believe that you have received it, and it will be yours." *~Mark 11:24*

"Now faith is confidence in what we hope for and assurance about what we do not see." *~ Hebrews 11:1*

"Because you know that the testing of your faith produces perseverance." *~James 1:3*

"I have chosen the way of faithfulness; I have set my heart on your laws." *~Psalms 119:30*

# Fame

"Keep your life free from love of money, and be content with what you have, for he has said, "I will never leave you nor forsake you." ~*Hebrews 13:5*

For "All flesh is like grass and all its glory like the flower of grass. The grass withers, and the flower falls." ~*1 Peter 1:24*

"Better is a poor person who walks in his integrity than one who is crooked in speech and is a fool." ~*Proverbs 19:1*

"Do not say, "I will do to him as he has done to me; I will pay the man back for what he has done." ~*Proverbs 24:29*

"For many, of whom I have often told you and now tell you even with tears, walk as enemies of the cross of Christ. Their end is destruction, their god is their belly, and they glory in their shame, with minds set on earthly things." *Philippians 3:18-19*

"Let all bitterness and wrath and anger and clamor and slander be put away from you, along with all malice. Be kind to one another, tenderhearted, forgiving one another, as God in Christ forgave you." *Ephesians 4:31-32*

"Do not love the world or the things in the world. If anyone loves the world, the love of the Father is not in him. For all that is in the world—the desires of the flesh and the desires of the eyes and pride in possessions—is not from the Father but is from the world." *~1 John 2:15-16*

# *Fear*

"Great peace has those who love your law, and nothing can make them stumble." ***Psalm 119:165***

"For I am convinced that neither death, nor life, nor angels, nor principalities, nor things present, nor things to come, nor powers, nor height, nor depth, nor any other created thing, will be able to separate us from the love of God, which is in Christ Jesus our Lord." ***~ Romans 8:38-39***

"Jesus said to her, "I am the resurrection and the life; he who believes in Me will live even if he dies, and everyone who lives and believes in Me will never die. Do you believe this?" ***~John 11:25-26***

"O DEATH, WHERE IS YOUR VICTORY? O DEATH, WHERE IS YOUR STING?" The sting of death is sin, and the power of sin is the law; but thanks be to God, who gives us the victory through our Lord Jesus Christ." ***~1 Corinthians 15:55-57***

# Finishing

"I have fought the good fight, I have finished the race, I have kept the faith." *~2 Timothy 4:7*

"But I do not account my life of any value nor as precious to myself, if only I may finish my course and the ministry that I received from the Lord Jesus, to testify to the gospel of the grace of God." *~Acts 20:24*

"Do you not know that in a race all the runners run, but only one receives the prize? So run that you may obtain it. Every athlete exercises self-control in all things. They do it to receive a perishable wreath, but we are imperishable. So I do not run aimlessly; I do not box as one beating the air. But I discipline my body and keep it under control, lest after preaching to others I myself should be disqualified." *~1 Corinthians 9:24-27*

"Therefore, since we are surrounded by so great a cloud of witnesses, let us also lay aside every weight, and sin which clings so closely, and let us run with endurance the race that is set before us." *~Hebrews 12:1*

"I press on toward the goal for the prize of the upward call of God in Christ Jesus." *~Philippians 3:14*

"So as to walk in a manner worthy of the Lord, fully pleasing to him, bearing fruit in every good work and increasing in the knowledge of God. May you be strengthened with all power, according to his glorious might, for all endurance and patience with joy, giving thanks to the Father, who has qualified you to share in the inheritance of the saints in light. He has delivered us from the domain of darkness and transferred us to the kingdom of his beloved Son, in whom we have redemption, the forgiveness of sins." ~ *Colossians 1:10-14*

"And I am sure of this, that he who began a good work in you will bring it to completion at the day of Jesus Christ." *~Philippians 1:6*

"Watch yourselves, so that you may not lose what we have worked for, but may win a full reward." *~2 John 1:8*

"Cast your burden on the Lord, and he shall sustain you: he shall never suffer the righteous to be moved." *~Psalms 55:22*

# Forgiveness

"Be kind to one another, tenderhearted, forgiving one another, as God in Christ forgave you." *~Ephesians 4:32*

"For if you forgive others their trespasses, your heavenly Father will also forgive you, but if you do not forgive others their trespasses, neither will your Father forgive your trespasses." *~Matthew 6:14-15*

"Judge not, and you will not be judged; condemn not, and you will not be condemned; forgive, and you will be forgiven." *~Luke 6:37*

"Bearing with one another and, if one has a complaint against another, forgiving each other; as the Lord has forgiven you, so you also must forgive." *~Colossians 3:13*

"Then Peter came up and said to him, "Lord, how often will my brother sin against me, and I forgive him? As many as seven times?" Jesus said to him, "I do not say to you seven times, but seventy times seven." *~Matthew 18:21-22*

"And whenever you stand praying, forgive, if you have anything against anyone, so that your Father also who is in heaven may forgive you your trespasses."*~ Mark 11:25*

"But I say to you who hear, Love your enemies, do good to those who hate you." *~Luke 6:27*

"Beloved, never avenge yourselves, but leave it to the wrath of God, for it is written, "Vengeance is mine, I will repay, says the Lord." *~ **Romans 12:19***

"Pay attention to yourselves! If your brother sins, rebuke him, and if he repents, forgive him, and if he sins against you seven times in the day, and turns to you seven times, saying, 'I repent,' you must forgive him." *~**Luke 17:3-4***

"Do not repay evil for evil or reviling for reviling, but on the contrary, bless, for to this you were called, that you may obtain a blessing." *~**1 Peter 3:9***

"But I say to you, Love your enemies and pray for those who persecute you." *~**Matthew 5:44***

"As each has received a gift, use it to serve one another, as good stewards of God's varied grace."~ *1 Peter 4:10*

"Having gifts that differ according to the grace given to us, let us use them: if prophecy, in proportion to our faith." *~Romans 12:6*

"As each has received a gift, use it to serve one another, as good stewards of God's varied grace: whoever speaks, as one who speaks oracles of God; whoever serves, as one who serves by the strength that God supplies—in order that in everything God may be glorified through Jesus Christ. To him belong glory and dominion forever and ever. Amen." *~1 Peter 4:10-11*

"Do not neglect the gift you have, which was given you by prophecy when the council of elders laid their hands on you." *~1 Timothy 4:14*

"Having gifts that differ according to the grace given to us, let us use them: if prophecy, in proportion to our faith; if service, in our serving; the one who teaches, in his teaching; the one who exhorts, in his exhortation; the one who contributes, in generosity; the one who leads, with zeal; the one who does acts of mercy, with cheerfulness." *~Romans 12:6-8*

"For it will be like a man going on a journey, who called his servants and entrusted to them his property. To one he gave five talents, to another

two, to another one, to each according to his ability. Then he went away. He who had received the five talents went at once and traded with them, and he made five talents more. So also he who had the two talents made two talents more. But he who had received the one talent went and dug in the ground and hid his master's money." *~Matthew 25:14-30*

"You are the light of the world. A city set on a hill cannot be hidden. Nor do people light a lamp and put it under a basket, but on a stand, and it gives light to all in the house. In the same way, let your light shine before others, so that they may see your good works and give glory to your Father who is in heaven." *~Matthew 5:14-16*

"Whatever you do, work heartily, as for the Lord and not for men, knowing that from the Lord you will receive the inheritance as your reward. You are serving the Lord Christ. For the wrongdoer will be paid back for the wrong he has done, and there is no partiality." *~Colossians 3:23-25*

"For this reason I remind you to fan into flame the gift of God, which is in you through the laying on of my hands." *~2 Timothy 1:6*

"For to everyone who has will more be given, and he will have an abundance. But from the one who has not, even what he has will be taken away." *~Matthew 25:29*

"A man's gift makes room for him and brings him before the great." *~Proverbs 18:16*

# Hate

"If anyone says, "I love God," and hates his brother, he is a liar; for he who does not love his brother whom he has seen cannot love God whom he has not seen." *~1 John 4:20*

"Hatred stirs up strife, but love covers all offenses."
*~Proverbs 10:12*

"Everyone who hates his brother is a murderer, and you know that no murderer has eternal life abiding in him." *~1 John 3:15*

"There are six things that the Lord hates, seven that are an abomination to him: haughty eyes, a lying tongue, and hands that shed innocent blood, a heart that devises wicked plans, feet that make haste to run to evil, a false witness who breathes out lies, and one who sows discord among brothers."
*~Proverbs 6:16-19*

"For this reason God gave them up to dishonorable passions. For their women exchanged natural relations for those that are contrary to nature; and the men likewise gave up natural relations with women and were consumed with passion for one another, men committing shameless acts with men and receiving in themselves the due penalty for their error." *~Romans 1:26-27*

"You shall not hate your brother in your heart, but you shall reason frankly with your neighbor, lest you incur sin because of him." *~Leviticus 19:17*

"Let no corrupting talk come out of your mouths, but only such as is good for building up, as fits the occasion, that it may give grace to those who hear." *~Ephesians 4:29*

"Love is patient and kind; love does not envy or boast; it is not arrogant or rude. It does not insist on its own way; it is not irritable or resentful; it does not rejoice at wrongdoing, but rejoices with the truth. Love bears all things, believes all things, hopes all things, and endures all things." *~1 Corinthians 13:4-7*

# Heart

"Create in me a clean heart and renew a right spirit within me." *~Psalms 51:10*

"As for that in the good soil, they are those who, hearing the word, hold it fast in an honest and good heart, and bear fruit with patience." *~Luke 8:15*

"Above all, keep loving one another earnestly, since love covers a multitude of sins." *~1 Peter 4:8*

"The good person out of his good treasure brings forth good, and the evil person out of his evil treasure brings forth evil." *~Matthew 12:35*

"But what comes out of the mouth proceeds from the heart, and this defiles a person. For out of the heart come evil thoughts, murder, adultery, sexual immorality, theft, false witness, slander. These are what defile a person. But to eat with unwashed hands does not defile anyone."*~ Matthew 15:18-20*

"So, whether you eat or drink, or whatever you do, do all to the glory of God." *~1 Corinthians 10:31*

"Your word is a lamp to my feet and a light to my path." *~Psalm 119:105*

"If we confess our sins, he is faithful and just to forgive us our sins and to cleanse us from all unrighteousness." *~1 John 1:9*

"Be kind to one another, tenderhearted, forgiving one another, as God in Christ forgave you." *~Ephesians 4:32*

"Finally, brothers, whatever is true, whatever is honorable, whatever is just, whatever is pure, whatever is lovely, whatever is commendable, if there is any excellence, if there is anything worthy of praise, think about these things." *~Philippians 4:8*

# *Help*

"Do not neglect to do good and to share what you have, for such sacrifices are pleasing to God."~ *Hebrews 13:16*

"Let each of you look not only to his own interests, but also to the interests of others." *~Philippians 2:4*

"Give, and it will be given to you. Good measure, pressed down, shaken together, running over, will be put into your lap. For with the measure you use it will be measured back to you." *~Luke 6:38*

"But if anyone has the world's goods and sees his brother in need, yet closes his heart against him, how does God's love abide in him?" *~1 John 3:17*

"For I was hungry and you gave me food, I was thirsty and you gave me drink, I was a stranger and you welcomed me, I was naked and you clothed me, I was sick and you visited me, I was in prison and you came to me.' Then the righteous will answer him, saying, 'Lord, when did we see you hungry and feed you, or thirsty and give you drink? And when did we see you a stranger and welcome you, or naked and clothe you? And when did we see you sick or in prison and visit you?" *~Matthew 25:35-40*

"What good is it, my brothers, if someone says he has faith but does not have works? Can that faith save him? If a brother or sister is poorly clothed and lacking in daily food, and one of you says to them, "Go in peace, be warmed and filled," without giving

them the things needed for the body, what good is that? So also faith by itself, if it does not have works, is dead." ~ *James 2:14-17*

"Bear one another's burdens, and so fulfill the law of Christ." ~*Galatians 6:2*

"This is my commandment, that you love one another as I have loved you." ~*John 15:12*

"In the same way, let your light shine before others, so that they may see your good works and give glory to your Father who is in heaven." ~*Matthew 5:16*

"Whoever is generous to the poor lends to the Lord, and he will repay him for his deed." ~*Proverbs 19:17*

# Humility

"Humble yourselves, therefore, under the mighty hand of God so that at the proper time he may exalt you." *~1 Peter 5:6*

"Do nothing from rivalry or conceit, but in humility count others more significant than yourselves. Let each of you look not only to his own interests, but also to the interests of others. Have this mind among yourselves, which is yours in Christ Jesus, who, though he was in the form of God, did not count equality with God a thing to be grasped, but made himself nothing, taking the form of a servant, being born in the likeness of men." *~Philippians 2:3-11*

"But he gives more grace. Therefore it says, "God opposes the proud, but gives grace to the humble." *~James 4:6*

"Whoever exalts himself will be humbled, and whoever humbles himself will be exalted." *~Matthew 23:12*

"If my people who are called by my name humble themselves, and pray and seek my face and turn from their wicked ways, then I will hear from heaven and will forgive their sin and heal their land." *~2 Chronicles 7:14*

"If I must boast, I will boast of the things that show my weakness." *~2 Corinthians 11:30*

"For by grace you have been saved through faith. And this is not your own doing; it is the gift of God, not a result of works, so that no one may boast."
*~Ephesians 2:8-9*

# Intelligence

"For by grace you have been saved through faith. And this is not your own doing; it is the gift of God, not a result of works, so that no one may boast." **~Ephesians 2:8-9**

**"**For to set the mind on the flesh is death, but to set the mind on the Spirit is life and peace." **~Romans 8:6**

"Therefore, if anyone is in Christ, he is a new creation. The old has passed away; behold, the new has come." **~2 Corinthians 5:17**

"Now we have received not the spirit of the world, but the Spirit who is from God, that we might understand the things freely given us by God." **~1 Corinthians 2:12**

"I do not nullify the grace of God, for if righteousness were through the law, then Christ died for no purpose." **~Galatians 2:21**

"Yet we know that a person is not justified by works of the law but through faith in Jesus Christ, so we also have believed in Christ Jesus, in order to be justified by faith in Christ and not by works of the law, because by works of the law no one will be justified. But if, in our endeavor to be justified in Christ, we too were found to be sinners, is Christ then a servant of sin? Certainly not! For if I rebuild what I tore down, I prove myself to be a transgressor. For through the law I died to the law, so that I

might live to God. I have been crucified with Christ. It is no longer I who live, but Christ who lives in me. And the life I now live in the flesh I live by faith in the Son of God, who loved me and gave himself for me." *~Galatians 2:16-21*

"Now I would remind you, brothers, of the gospel I preached to you, which you received, in which you stand, and by which you are being saved, if you hold fast to the word I preached to you—unless you believed in vain." *~1 Corinthians 15:1-2*

"For those whom he foreknew he also predestined to be conformed to the image of his Son, in order that he might be the firstborn among many brothers." *Romans 8:29*

"You, however, are not in the flesh but in the Spirit, if in fact the Spirit of God dwells in you. Anyone who does not have the Spirit of Christ does not belong to him." *~Romans 8:9*

"Therefore, as one trespass led to condemnation for all men, so one act of righteousness leads to justification and life for all men." *~ Romans 5:18*

*Intuition*

"For the word of God is living and active, sharper than any two-edged sword, piercing to the division of soul and of spirit, of joints and of marrow, and discerning the thoughts and intentions of the heart." *~Hebrews 4:12*

"That the God of our Lord Jesus Christ, the Father of glory, may give you a spirit of wisdom and of revelation in the knowledge of him." *~Ephesians 1:17*

"All Scripture is breathed out by God and profitable for teaching, for reproof, for correction, and for training in righteousness." *~2 Timothy 3:16*

"For "'In him we live and move and have our being'; as even some of your own poets have said, "For we are indeed his offspring."'*~ Acts 17:28*

"I have said these things to you, that in me you may have peace. In the world you will have tribulation. But take heart; I have overcome the world."*~ John 16:33*

"God is spirit, and those who worship him must worship in spirit and truth."*~ John 4:24*

"Go therefore and make disciples of all nations, baptizing them in the name of the Father and of the Son and of the Holy Spirit." *~Matthew 28:19*

"Praise the Lord! Praise the Lord from the heavens; praise him in the heights! Praise him, all his angels; praise him, all his hosts! Praise him, sun and moon; praise him, all you shining stars! Praise him, you highest heavens, and you waters above the heavens! Let them praise the name of the Lord! For he commanded and they were created." *~Psalm 148:1-14*

"If a prophet or a dreamer of dreams arises among you and gives you a sign or a wonder, and the sign or wonder that he tells you comes to pass, and if he says, 'Let us go after other gods,' which you have not known, 'and let us serve them,' you shall not listen to the words of that prophet or that dreamer of dreams. For the Lord your God is testing you, to know whether you love the Lord your God with all your heart and with all your soul. You shall walk after the Lord your God and fear him and keep his commandments and obey his voice, and you shall serve him and hold fast to him. But that prophet or that dreamer of dreams shall be put to death, because he has taught rebellion against the Lord your God, who brought you out of the land of Egypt and redeemed you out of the house of slavery, to make you leave the way in which the Lord your God commanded you to walk. So you shall purge the evil from your midst." *~ Deuteronomy 13:1-18*

*Jesus*

"Now faith is the assurance of things hoped for, the conviction of things not seen."~ ***Hebrews 11:1***

"And without faith it is impossible to please him, for whoever would draw near to God must believe that he exists and that he rewards those who seek him." ***Hebrews 11:6***

"For by grace you have been saved through faith. And this is not your own doing; it is the gift of God." ***Ephesians 2:8***

"Looking to Jesus, the founder and perfecter of our faith, who for the joy that was set before him endured the cross, despising the shame, and is seated at the right hand of the throne of God." ***~Hebrews 12:2***

"So faith comes from hearing, and hearing through the word of Christ." ***~ Romans 10:17***

"Yet we know that a person is not justified by works of the law but through faith in Jesus Christ, so we also have believed in Christ Jesus, in order to be justified by faith in Christ and not by works of the law, because by works of the law no one will be justified." ***~Galatians 2:16***

"I have been crucified with Christ. It is no longer I who live, but Christ who lives in me. And the life I now live in the flesh I live by faith in the Son of God, who loved me and gave himself for me." ~**Galatians 2:20**

"For we are his workmanship, created in Christ Jesus for good works, which God prepared beforehand, that we should walk in them." ~**Ephesians 2:10**

# Joy

Rejoice in hope, be patient in tribulation, be constant in prayer. *~Romans 12:12*

Count it all joy, my brothers, when you meet trials of various kinds, *~James 1:2*

May the God of hope fill you with all joy and peace in believing, so that by the power of the Holy Spirit you may abound in hope. *~Romans 15:13*

Rejoice in the Lord always; again I will say, Rejoice. *~Philippians 4:4*

But the fruit of the Spirit is love, joy, peace, patience, kindness, goodness, faithfulness, *~Galatians 5:22*

Until now you have asked nothing in my name. Ask, and you will receive, that your joy may be full. *~John 16:24*

Though you have not seen him, you love him. Though you do not now see him, you believe in him and rejoice with joy that is inexpressible and filled with glory, *~1 Peter 1:8*

A joyful heart is good medicine, but a crushed spirit dries up the bones. *~Proverbs 17:22*

# Judgment

For judgment is without mercy to one who has shown no mercy. Mercy triumphs over judgment. *~James 2:13*

So then each of us will give an account of himself to God. Therefore let us not pass judgment on one another any longer, but rather decide never to put a stumbling block or hindrance in the way of a brother. *~Romans 14:12-13*

Why do you pass judgment on your brother? Or you, why do you despise your brother? For we will all stand before the judgment seat of God; for it is written, "As I live, says the Lord, every knee shall bow to me, and every tongue shall confess to God." So then each of us will give an account of himself to God. *~Romans 14:10-12*

Therefore do not pronounce judgment before the time, before the Lord comes, who will bring to light the things now hidden in darkness and will disclose the purposes of the heart. Then each one will receive his commendation from God. *~1 Corinthians 4:5*

"For by your words you will be justified, and by your words you will be condemned." *~Matthew 12:37*

"By this is love perfected with us, so that we may have confidence for the day of judgment, because as he is so also are we in this world." *~1 John 4:17*

*Kindness*

"Be kind to one another, tender-hearted, forgiving each other, just as God in Christ also has forgiven you." ~ *Ephesians 4:32*

"For God is not unjust so as to forget your work and the love which you have shown toward His name, in having ministered and in still ministering to the saints." ~ *Hebrews 6:10*

"Or do you think lightly of the riches of His kindness and tolerance and patience, not knowing that the kindness of God leads you to repentance?" ~ *Romans 2:4*

But the fruit of the Spirit is love, joy, peace, patience, kindness, goodness, faithfulness, gentleness, self-control; against such things there is no law. ~ *Galatians 5:22-23*

"But love your enemies, and do good, and lend, expecting nothing in return; and your reward will be great, and you will be sons of the Most High; for He Himself is kind to ungrateful and evil men." ~ *Luke 6:35*

"So, as those who have been chosen of God, holy and beloved, put on a heart of compassion, kindness, humility, gentleness and patience;" ~ *Colossians 3:12*

"But the fruit of the Spirit is love, joy, peace, patience, kindness, goodness, faithfulness" ~ *Galatians 5:22*

"Do not let kindness and truth leave you; Bind them around your neck, Write them on the tablet of your heart." ~ *Proverbs 3:3*

"And we know that God causes all things to work together for good to those who love God, to those who are called according to His purpose." ~ *Romans 8:28*

"Do not neglect to show hospitality to strangers, for by this some have entertained angels without knowing it." ~ *Hebrews 13:2*

# *Legacy*

"We will not hide them from their children, but tell to the coming generation the glorious deeds of the Lord, and his might, and the wonders that he has done." *~Psalm 78:4*

"You shall love the Lord your God with all your heart and with all your soul and with all your might. And these words that I command you today shall be on your heart. You shall teach them diligently to your children, and shall talk of them when you sit in your house, and when you walk by the way, and when you lie down, and when you rise." *~Deuteronomy 6:5-7*

"And what you have heard from me in the presence of many witnesses entrust to faithful men who will be able to teach others also." *~2 Timothy 2:2*

"I charge you in the presence of God and of Christ Jesus, who is to judge the living and the dead, and by his appearing and his kingdom: preach the word; be ready in season and out of season; reprove, rebuke, and exhort, with complete patience and teaching. For the time is coming when people will not endure sound teaching, but having itching ears they will accumulate for themselves teachers to suit their own passions, and will turn away from listening to the truth and wander off into myths. As for you, always be sober-minded, endure suffering, do the work of an evangelist, fulfill your ministry." *~2 Timothy 4:1-22*

"But the steadfast love of the Lord is from everlasting to everlasting on those who fear him, and his righteousness to children's children" *~Psalm 103:17*

"You shall not bow down to them or serve them, for I the Lord your God am a jealous God, visiting the iniquity of the fathers on the children to the third and the fourth generation of those who hate me, but showing steadfast love to thousands of those who love me and keep my commandments." *~Exodus 20:5-6*

# Loneliness

"Fear not, for I am with you; be not dismayed, for I am your God; I will strengthen you, I will help you, I will uphold you with my righteous right hand."
**~Isaiah 41:10**

"Casting all your anxieties on him, because he cares for you." **~1 Peter 5:7**

"No man shall be able to stand before you all the days of your life. Just as I was with Moses, so I will be with you. I will not leave you or forsake you."
**~Joshua 1:5**

"Even though I walk through the valley of the shadow of death, I will fear no evil, for you are with me; your rod and your staff, they comfort me."
**~Psalm 23:4**

"Be strong and courageous. Do not fear or be in dread of them, for it is the Lord your God who goes with you. He will not leave you or forsake you."
**~Deuteronomy 31:6**

"Then the Lord God said, "It is not good that the man should be alone; I will make him a helper fit for him."**~ Genesis 2:18**

"Teaching them to observe all that I have commanded you. And behold, I am with you always, to the end of the age." **~Matthew 28:20**

"Do not be anxious about anything, but in everything by prayer and supplication with thanksgiving let your requests be made known to God. And the peace of God, which surpasses all understanding, will guard your hearts and your minds in Christ Jesus." *~Philippians 4:6-7*

"Who shall separate us from the love of Christ? Shall tribulation, or distress, or persecution, or famine, or nakedness, or danger, or sword? As it is written, "For your sake we are being killed all the day long; we are regarded as sheep to be slaughtered." No, in all these things we are more than conquerors through him who loved us. For I am sure that neither death nor life, nor angels nor rulers, nor things present nor things to come, nor powers, nor height nor depth, nor anything else in all creation, will be able to separate us from the love of God in Christ Jesus our Lord." *~Romans 8:35-39*

# Love

"Love is patient, love is kind. It does not envy, it does not boast, it is not proud. It does not dishonor others, it is not self-seeking, it is not easily angered, it keeps no record of wrongs. Love does not delight in evil but rejoices with the truth. It always protects, always trusts, always hopes, always perseveres." *~1 Corinthians 13:4-7*

"Whoever does not love does not know God, because God is love." *~1 John 4:8*

"Dear friends, let us love one another, for love comes from God. Everyone who loves has been born of God and knows God. Whoever does not love does not know God, because God is love. This is how God showed his love among us: He sent his one and only Son into the world that we might live through him. This is love: not that we loved God, but that he loved us and sent his Son as an atoning sacrifice for our sins." *~1 John 4:7-10*

"For God so loved the world that he gave his one and only Son,[a] that whoever believes in him shall not perish but have eternal life." *~ John 3:16*

"Know therefore that the LORD your God is God; he is the faithful God, keeping his covenant of love to a thousand generations of those who love him and keep his commands." *~ Deuteronomy 7:9*

"This is how God showed his love among us: He sent his one and only Son into the world that we might live through him. This is love: not that we loved God, but that he loved us and sent his Son as an atoning sacrifice for our sins. Dear friends, since God so loved us, we also ought to love one another." *~ 1 John 4:9-11*

"And so we know and rely on the love God has for us. God is love. Whoever lives in love lives in God, and God in him." *~ 1 John 4:16*

"We love because he first loved us. If anyone says, "I love God," yet hates his brother, he is a liar. For anyone who does not love his brother, whom he has seen, cannot love God, whom he has not seen." *~ 1 John 4:19-20*

# Miracles

"While you stretch out your hand to heal, and signs and wonders are performed through the name of your holy servant Jesus." *~Acts 4:30*

"So Jesus said to him, "Unless you see signs and wonders you will not believe." *~John 4:48*

"And his name—by faith in his name—has made this man strong whom you see and know, and the faith that is through Jesus has given the man this perfect health in the presence of you all." *~Acts 3:16*

"Truly, truly, I say to you, whoever believes in me will also do the works that I do; and greater works than these will he do, because I am going to the Father." *~John 14:12*

"And these signs will accompany those who believe: in my name they will cast out demons; they will speak in new tongues;" *~Mark 16:17*

"The coming of the lawless one is by the activity of Satan with all power and false signs and wonders." *~2 Thessalonians 2:9*

"And God was doing extraordinary miracles by the hands of Paul." *~Acts 19:11*

"He said to them, "Because of your little faith. For truly, I say to you, if you have faith like a grain of mustard seed, you will say to this mountain, 'Move from here to there,' and it will move, and nothing will be impossible for you." *~Matthew 17:20*

"And there was a woman who had had a discharge of blood for twelve years, and though she had spent all her living on physicians, she could not be healed by anyone. She came up behind him and touched the fringe of his garment, and immediately her discharge of blood ceased. And Jesus said, "Who was it that touched me?" When all denied it, Peter said, "Master, the crowds surround you and are pressing in on you!" But Jesus said, "Someone touched me, for I perceive that power has gone out from me." And when the woman saw that she was not hidden, she came trembling, and falling down before him declared in the presence of all the people why she had touched him, and how she had been immediately healed." *~Luke 8:43-48*

"So they remained for a long time, speaking boldly for the Lord, who bore witness to the word of his grace, granting signs and wonders to be done by their hands." *~Acts 14:3*

"Jesus said to her, "Did I not tell you that if you believed you would see the glory of God?" So they took away the stone. And Jesus lifted up his eyes and said, "Father, I thank you that you have heard me. I knew that you always hear me, but I said this on account of the people standing around, that they may believe that you sent me." *~ John 11:40-42*

"By the power of signs and wonders, by the power of the Spirit of God—so that from Jerusalem and all the way around to Illyricum I have fulfilled the ministry of the gospel of Christ" *~Romans 15:19*

# Negotiation

"All the ways of a man are pure in his own eyes, but the Lord weighs the spirit." **~Proverbs 16:2**

"What causes quarrels and what causes fights among you? Is it not this, that your passions are at war within you? You desire and do not have, so you murder. You covet and cannot obtain, so you fight and quarrel. You do not have, because you do not ask." **~James 4:1-2**

"Let every person be subject to the governing authorities. For there is no authority except from God, and those that exist have been instituted by God. Therefore whoever resists the authorities resists what God has appointed, and those who resist will incur judgment. For rulers are not a terror to good conduct, but to bad. Would you have no fear of the one who is in authority? Then do what is good, and you will receive his approval, for he is God's servant for your good. But if you do wrong, be afraid, for he does not bear the sword in vain. For he is the servant of God, an avenger who carries out God's wrath on the wrongdoer. Therefore one must be in subjection, not only to avoid God's wrath but also for the sake of conscience." **~Romans 13:1-7**

"So, whether you eat or drink, or whatever you do, do all to the glory of God." **~1 Corinthians 10:31**

"A time to love, and a time to hate; a time for war, and a time for peace." **~Ecclesiastes 3:8**

"And Hannah prayed and said, "My heart exults in the Lord; my strength is exalted in the Lord. My mouth derides my enemies, because I rejoice in your salvation. "There is none holy like the Lord; there is none besides you; there is no rock like our God. Talk no more so very proudly, let not arrogance come from your mouth; for the Lord is a God of knowledge, and by him actions are weighed. The bows of the mighty are broken, but the feeble bind on strength. Those who were full have hired themselves out for bread, but those who were hungry have ceased to hunger. The barren has borne seven, but she who has many children is forlorn." ~ *1 Samuel 2:1-36*

# Obstacles

"And we know that for those who love God all things work together for good, for those who are called according to his purpose." *~Romans 8:28*

"Three times I pleaded with the Lord about this, that it should leave me. But he said to me, "My grace is sufficient for you, for my power is made perfect in weakness." Therefore I will boast all the more gladly of my weaknesses, so that the power of Christ may rest upon me. For the sake of Christ, then, I am content with weaknesses, insults, hardships, persecutions, and calamities. For when I am weak, then I am strong." *~2 Corinthians 12:8-10*

"I appeal to you, brothers, to watch out for those who cause divisions and create obstacles contrary to the doctrine that you have been taught; avoid them." *~Romans 16:17*

"More than that, we rejoice in our sufferings, knowing that suffering produces endurance, and endurance produces character, and character produces hope, and hope does not put us to shame, because God's love has been poured into our hearts through the Holy Spirit who has been given to us." *~Romans 5:3-5*

"Count it all joy, my brothers, when you meet trials of various kinds, for you know that the testing of your faith produces steadfastness. And let steadfastness have its full effect, that you may be perfect and complete, lacking in nothing." *~James 1:2-4*

"He said to them, "Because of your little faith. For truly, I say to you, if you have faith like a grain of mustard seed, you will say to this mountain, 'Move from here to there,' and it will move, and nothing will be impossible for you." *~Matthew 17:20*

"And it shall be said, "Build up, build up, prepare the way, remove every obstruction from my people's way." *~Isaiah 57:14*

"We put no obstacle in anyone's way, so that no fault may be found with our ministry." *~2 Corinthians 6:3*

"I can do all things through him who strengthens me." *~Philippians 4:13*

"For still the vision awaits its appointed time; it hastens to the end—it will not lie. If it seems slow, wait for it; it will surely come; it will not delay." *~Habakkuk 2:3*

"If others share this rightful claim on you, do not we even more? Nevertheless, we have not made use of this right, but we endure anything rather than put an obstacle in the way of the gospel of Christ." *~1 Corinthians 9:12*

"Judge not, that you be not judged. For with the judgment you pronounce you will be judged, and with the measure you use it will be measured to you. Why do you see the speck that is in your brother's eye, but do not notice the log that is in your own eye? Or how can you say to your brother, 'Let me take the speck out of your eye,' when there is the log in your own eye? You hypocrite, first take the log out of your own eye, and then you will see clearly to take the speck out of your brother's eye." *~Matthew 7:1-29*

"Do not be anxious about anything, but in everything by prayer and supplication with thanksgiving let your requests be made known to God." *~Philippians 4:6*

# Patience

"Rejoice in hope, be patient in tribulation, be constant in prayer." ***~Romans 12:12***

"But if we hope for what we do not see, we wait for it with patience." ***~Romans 8:25***

"And let us not grow weary of doing good, for in due season we will reap, if we do not give up." ***~Galatians 6:9***

"Be still before the Lord and wait patiently for him; fret not yourself over the one who prospers in his way, over the man who carries out evil devices! Refrain from anger, and forsake wrath! Fret not yourself; it tends only to evil. For the evildoers shall be cut off, but those who wait for the Lord shall inherit the land." ***~Psalm 37:7-9***

"Do not be anxious about anything, but in everything by prayer and supplication with thanksgiving let your requests be made known to God." ***~Philippians 4:6***

"For I know the plans I have for you, declares the Lord, plans for welfare and not for evil, to give you a future and a hope." ***~Jeremiah 29:11***

"Be not quick in your spirit to become angry, for anger lodges in the bosom of fools." ***Ecclesiastes 7:9***

"With all humility and gentleness, with patience, bearing with one another in love." *~Ephesians 4:2*

"And endurance produces character, and character produces hope." *~Romans 5:4*

"Know this, my beloved brothers: let every person be quick to hear, slow to speak, slow to anger." *~James 1:19*

"But they who wait for the Lord shall renew their strength; they shall mount up with wings like eagles; they shall run and not be weary; they shall walk and not faint." *~Isaiah 40:31*

"For you know that the testing of your faith produces steadfastness." *~James 1:3*

# Peace

"Peace I leave with you; my peace I give to you. Not as the world gives do I give to you. Let not your hearts be troubled, neither let them be afraid." *~John 14:27*

"I have said these things to you, that in me you may have peace. In the world you will have tribulation. But take heart; I have overcome the world." *~John 16:33*

"You keep him in perfect peace whose mind is stayed on you, because he trusts in you." *~Isaiah 26:3*

"The God of peace will soon crush Satan under your feet. The grace of our Lord Jesus Christ be with you." *~Romans 16:20*

"May the God of hope fill you with all joy and peace in believing, so that by the power of the Holy Spirit you may abound in hope." *~Romans 15:13*

"Ask, and it will be given to you; seek, and you will find; knock, and it will be opened to you." *~Matthew 7:7*

"Therefore, since we have been justified by faith, we have peace with God through our Lord Jesus Christ." *~Romans 5:1*

"Fear not, for I am with you; be not dismayed, for I am your God; I will strengthen you, I will help you, I will uphold you with my righteous right hand." **~Isaiah 41:10**

ESV / 52 helpful votes

"Strive for peace with everyone, and for the holiness without which no one will see the Lord." **~Hebrews 12:14**

"Cast your burden on the Lord, and he will sustain you; he will never permit the righteous to be moved." **~Psalm 55:22**

"A Psalm of David. The Lord is my shepherd; I shall not want. He makes me lie down in green pastures. He leads me beside still waters. He restores my soul. He leads me in paths of righteousness for his name's sake. Even though I walk through the valley of the shadow of death, I will fear no evil, for you are with me; your rod and your staff, they comfort me. You prepare a table before me in the presence of my enemies; you anoint my head with oil; my cup overflows." **~ Psalm 23:1-6**

"Whoever speaks, as one who speaks oracles of God; whoever serves, as one who serves by the strength that God supplies—in order that in everything God may be glorified through Jesus Christ. To him belong glory and dominion forever and ever. Amen." *~1 Peter 4:11*

"But in your hearts honor Christ the Lord as holy, always being prepared to make a defense to anyone who asks you for a reason for the hope that is in you; yet do it with gentleness and respect." *~1 Peter 3:15*

"I can do all things through him who strengthens me." *~ Philippians 4:13*

"Finally, be strong in the Lord and in the strength of his might." *~ Ephesians 6:10*

"Teaching them to observe all that I have commanded you. And behold, I am with you always, to the end of the age." *~Matthew 28:20*

"But Jesus looked at them and said, "With man this is impossible, but with God all things are possible."*~ Matthew 19:26*

He said to them, "Because of your little faith. For truly, I say to you, if you have faith like a grain of mustard seed, you will say to this mountain, 'Move from here to there,' and it will move, and nothing will be impossible for you." *~Matthew 17:20*

"The Lord your God is in your midst, a mighty one who will save; he will rejoice over you with gladness; he will quiet you by his love; he will exult over you with loud singing." *~Zephaniah 3:17*

# Quiet

"The Lord will fight for you, and you have only to be silent." ***~Exodus 14:14***

"He made the storm be still, and the waves of the sea were hushed." ***~Psalm 107:29***

"The wise of heart will receive commandments, but a babbling fool will come to ruin." ***~Proverbs 10:8***

But Joshua commanded the people, "You shall not shout or make your voice heard, neither shall any word go out of your mouth, until the day I tell you to shout. Then you shall shout." ***~Joshua 6:10***

"Whoever belittles his neighbor lacks sense, but a man of understanding remains silent." ***~Proverbs 11:12***

"Let all bitterness and wrath and anger and clamor and slander be put away from you, along with all malice." ***~Ephesians 4:31***

"A soft answer turns away wrath, but a harsh word stirs up anger." ***~Proverbs 15:1***

"To speak evil of no one, to avoid quarreling, to be gentle, and to show perfect courtesy toward all people." ***~Titus 3:2***

"Cease to hear instruction, my son, and you will stray from the words of knowledge." ***~Proverbs 19:27***

"The way of a fool is right in his own eyes, but a wise man listens to advice." **~Proverbs 12:15**

"Where there is no guidance, a people falls, but in an abundance of counselors there is safety." **~Proverbs 11:14**

"I can do all things through him who strengthens me." **~Philippians 4:13**

"But I do not account my life of any value nor as precious to myself, if only I may finish my course and the ministry that I received from the Lord Jesus, to testify to the gospel of the grace of God." ***~Acts 20:24***

"And I will ask the Father, and he will give you another Helper, to be with you forever." ***~John 14:16***

"Your word is a lamp to my feet and a light to my path." ***~Psalm 119:105***

"The Lord is not slow to fulfill his promise as some count slowness, but is patient toward you, not wishing that any should perish, but that all should reach repentance." ***~2 Peter 3:9***

"Or do you not know that the unrighteous will not inherit the kingdom of God? Do not be deceived: neither the sexually immoral, nor idolaters, nor adulterers, nor men who practice homosexuality, nor thieves, nor the greedy, nor drunkards, nor revilers, nor swindlers will inherit the kingdom of God. And such were some of you. But you were washed, you were sanctified, you were justified in the name of the Lord Jesus Christ and by the Spirit of our God." *~1 Corinthians 6:9-11*

"Therefore, since we have been justified by faith, we have peace with God through our Lord Jesus Christ." *~Romans 5:1*

"What then shall we say to these things? If God is for us, who can be against us?~ **Romans 8:31**

"When the righteous cry for help, the Lord hears and delivers them out of all their troubles. The Lord is near to the brokenhearted and saves the crushed in spirit. Many are the afflictions of the righteous, but the Lord delivers him out of them all. He keeps all his bones; not one of them is broken." **~Psalm 34:17-20**

"If the world hates you, know that it has hated me before it hated you." **~John 15:18**

But he said to me, "My grace is sufficient for you, for my power is made perfect in weakness." Therefore I will boast all the more gladly of my weaknesses, so that the power of Christ may rest upon me. **~2 Corinthians 12:9**

"For the Lord will not forsake his people; he will not abandon his heritage." **~Psalm 94:14**

"He was despised and rejected by men; a man of sorrows, and acquainted with grief; and as one from whom men hide their faces he was despised, and we esteemed him not." **~Isaiah 53:3**

"He came to his own, and his own people did not receive him." **~John 1:11**

"Casting all your anxieties on him, because he cares for you." *~1 Peter 5:7*

"The one who hears you hears me, and the one who rejects you rejects me, and the one who rejects me rejects him who sent me." *~Luke 10:16*

"There is therefore now no condemnation for those who are in Christ Jesus." *~Romans 8:1*

"Be sober-minded; be watchful. Your adversary the devil prowls around like a roaring lion, seeking someone to devour." *~1 Peter 5:8*

"And my God will supply every need of yours according to his riches in glory in Christ Jesus." *~Philippians 4:19*

# Righteousness

"If you know that he is righteous, you may be sure that everyone who practices righteousness has been born of him." *~1 John 2:29*

"Therefore, since we have been justified by faith, we have peace with God through our Lord Jesus Christ. Through him we have also obtained access by faith into this grace in which we stand, and we rejoice in hope of the glory of God. More than that, we rejoice in our sufferings, knowing that suffering produces endurance, and endurance produces character, and character produces hope, and hope does not put us to shame, because God's love has been poured into our hearts through the Holy Spirit who has been given to us." *~Romans 5:1-5*

"Blessed are they who observe justice, who do righteousness at all times!" *~Psalm 106:3*

He who walks righteously and speaks uprightly, who despises the gain of oppressions, who shakes his hands, lest they hold a bribe, who stops his ears from hearing of bloodshed and shuts his eyes from looking on evil, he will dwell on the heights; his place of defense will be the fortresses of rocks; his bread will be given him; his water will be sure. Your eyes will behold the king in his beauty; they will see a land that stretches afar. *~ Isaiah 33:15-17*

"Filled with the fruit of righteousness that comes through Jesus Christ, to the glory and praise of God." *~Philippians 1:11*

"For Christ is the end of the law for righteousness to everyone who believes." *~Romans 10:4*

"So flee youthful passions and pursue righteousness, faith, love, and peace, along with those who call on the Lord from a pure heart." *~2 Timothy 2:22*

# Self Esteem

"Do not let your adorning be external—the braiding of hair and the putting on of gold jewelry, or the clothing you wear— but let your adorning be the hidden person of the heart with the imperishable beauty of a gentle and quiet spirit, which in God's sight is very precious." *~1 Peter 3:3-4*

"For you formed my inward parts; you knitted me together in my mother's womb. I praise you, for I am fearfully and wonderfully made. Wonderful are your works; my soul knows it very well." *~Psalm 139:13-14*

"For I know the plans I have for you, declares the Lord, plans for welfare and not for evil, to give you a future and a hope." *~Jeremiah 29:11*

"Come to me, all who labor and are heavy laden, and I will give you rest. Take my yoke upon you, and learn from me, for I am gentle and lowly in heart, and you will find rest for your souls. For my yoke is easy, and my burden is light." *~Matthew 11:28-30*

"There is therefore now no condemnation for those who are in Christ Jesus. For the law of the Spirit of life has set you free in Christ Jesus from the law of sin and death." *~Romans 8:1-2*

"And he said to them, "You are those who justify yourselves before men, but God knows your hearts. For what is exalted among men is an abomination in the sight of God." *~Luke 16:15*

"Then God said, "Let us make man in our image, after our likeness. And let them have dominion over the fish of the sea and over the birds of the heavens and over the livestock and over all the earth and over every creeping thing that creeps on the earth." So God created man in his own image, in the image of God he created him; male and female he created them." *~Genesis 1:26-27*

"Before I formed you in the womb I knew you, and before you were born I consecrated you; I appointed you a prophet to the nations." *~Jeremiah 1:5*

"And if I go and prepare a place for you, I will come again and will take you to myself, that where I am you may be also. And you know the way to where I am going." *~John 14:3-4*

*Talent*

"Having gifts that differ according to the grace given to us, let us use them: if prophecy, in proportion to our faith." ~ **Romans 12:6**

"Every good gift and every perfect gift is from above, coming down from the Father of lights with whom there is no variation or shadow due to change." **~James 1:17**

"As each has received a gift, use it to serve one another, as good stewards of God's varied grace." **~1 Peter 4:10**

"Let every skillful craftsman among you come and make all that the Lord has commanded." **~Exodus 35:10**

"And I have filled him with the Spirit of God, with ability and intelligence, with knowledge and all craftsmanship, to devise artistic designs, to work in gold, silver, and bronze, in cutting stones for setting, and in carving wood, to work in every craft." **~Exodus 31:3-5**

"When the day of Pentecost arrived, they were all together in one place. And suddenly there came from heaven a sound like a mighty rushing wind, and it filled the entire house where they were sitting. And divided tongues as of fire appeared to them and rested on each one of them. And they were all filled with the Holy Spirit and began to speak in other tongues as the Spirit gave them utterance. Now there were dwelling in Jerusalem Jews, devout men from every nation under heaven." *~Acts 2:1-47*

"Let all that you do be done in love." *~1 Corinthians 16:14*

# Trust

"Trust in the Lord with all your heart, and do not lean on your own understanding." *~Proverbs 3:5*

"When I am afraid, I put my trust in you. In God, whose word I praise, in God I trust; I shall not be afraid. What can flesh do to me?" *~Psalm 56:3-4 .*

"There is no fear in love, but perfect love casts out fear. For fear has to do with punishment, and whoever fears has not been perfected in love." *~1 John 4:18*

"But I have trusted in your steadfast love; my heart shall rejoice in your salvation." *~Psalm 13:5*

"Blessed is the man who makes the Lord his trust, who does not turn to the proud, to those who go astray after a lie!" *~Psalm 40:4*

"Therefore I tell you, whatever you ask in prayer, believe that you have received it, and it will be yours." *~Mark 11:24*

"Commit your way to the Lord; trust in him, and he will act." *~Psalm 37:5*

"But I trust in you, O Lord; I say, "You are my God." My times are in your hand; rescue me from the hand of my enemies and from my persecutors!" *~Psalm 31:14-15*

"In all your ways acknowledge him, and he will make straight your paths." *~Proverbs 3:6*

"Do not be conformed to this world, but be transformed by the renewal of your mind, that by testing you may discern what is the will of God, what is good and acceptable and perfect." *~Romans 12:2*

# Understanding

"The unfolding of your words gives light; it imparts understanding to the simple." *~Psalm 119:130*

"A fool takes no pleasure in understanding, but only in expressing his opinion." *~Proverbs 18:2*

"Making your ear attentive to wisdom and inclining your heart to understanding; yes, if you call out for insight and raise your voice for understanding, if you seek it like silver and search for it as for hidden treasures, then you will understand the fear of the Lord and find the knowledge of God." *~Proverbs 2:2-5*

"Whoever restrains his words has knowledge, and he who has a cool spirit is a man of understanding." *~Proverbs 17:27*

"Let your speech always be gracious, seasoned with salt, so that you may know how you ought to answer each person." *~Colossians 4:6*

"The beginning of wisdom is this: Get wisdom, and whatever you get, get insight." *~Proverbs 4:7*

# Victim

"No temptation has overtaken you that is not common to man. God is faithful, and he will not let you be tempted beyond your ability, but with the temptation he will also provide the way of escape, that you may be able to endure it." *~1 Corinthians 10:13*

"Put to death therefore what is earthly in you: sexual immorality, impurity, passion, evil desire, and covetousness, which is idolatry." *~ Colossians 3:5*

"Or do you not know that your body is a temple of the Holy Spirit within you, whom you have from God? You are not your own." *~ 1 Corinthians 6:19*

"For he is God's servant for your good. But if you do wrong, be afraid, for he does not bear the sword in vain. For he is the servant of God, an avenger who carries out God's wrath on the wrongdoer." *~ Romans 13:4*

"And saying, "The time is fulfilled, and the kingdom of God is at hand; repent and believe in the gospel."*~ Mark 1:15*

"And when the thousand years are ended, Satan will be released from his prison and will come out to deceive the nations that are at the four corners of the earth, Gog and Magog, to gather them for battle; their number is like the sand of the sea. And they marched up over the broad plain of the earth and surrounded the camp of the saints and the beloved city, but fire came down from heaven and consumed them." *~ **Revelation 20:7-9***

# *Winning*

"For with God nothing shall be impossible." ~ *Luke 1:37*

"For everyone who has been born of God overcomes the world. And this is the victory that has overcome the world—our faith. Who is it that overcomes the world except the one who believes that Jesus is the Son of God?" ~ *1 John 5:4-5*

"I can do all things through him who strengthens me." ~*Philippians 4:13*

"Every athlete exercises self-control in all things. They do it to receive a perishable wreath, but we are imperishable." ~ *1 Corinthians 9:25*

But he said, "What is impossible with men is possible with God." ~*Luke 18:27*

*Hebrews 12:1-2* ESV / 18 helpful votes  - Therefore, since we are surrounded by so great a cloud of witnesses, let us also lay aside every weight, and sin which clings so closely, and let us run with endurance the race that is set before us, looking to Jesus, the founder and perfecter of our faith, who for the joy that was set before him endured the cross, despising the shame, and is seated at the right hand of the throne of God.

"But thanks be to God, who gives us the victory through our Lord Jesus Christ." ~*1 Corinthians 15:57*

"So the last will be first, and the first last." ~ **Matthew 20:16**

"Light dawns in the darkness for the upright; he is gracious, merciful, and righteous." ~**Psalm 112:4**

"And the king's young men told him, "Haman is there, standing in the court." And the king said, "Let him come in." ~**Esther 6:5**

"Remember not the former things, nor consider the things of old. Behold, I am doing a new thing; now it springs forth, do you not perceive it? I will make a way in the wilderness and rivers in the desert." *~Isaiah 43:18-19*

"Not that I have already obtained this or am already perfect, but I press on to make it my own, because Christ Jesus has made me his own. Brothers, I do not consider that I have made it my own. But one thing I do: forgetting what lies behind and straining forward to what lies ahead, I press on toward the goal for the prize of the upward call of God in Christ Jesus." *~Philippians 3:12-14*

"Submit yourselves therefore to God. Resist the devil, and he will flee from you." *~James 4:7*

"You who have made me see many troubles and calamities will revive me again; from the depths of the earth you will bring me up again." *~Psalm 71:20*

"Who gave himself for our sins to deliver us from the present evil age, according to the will of our God and Father." *~Galatians 1:4*

# Yesterday

"Jesus Christ is the same yesterday and today and forever." *~ Hebrews 13:8*

"All Scripture is breathed out by God and profitable for teaching, for reproof, for correction, and for training in righteousness." *~2 Timothy 3:16*

"And you will know the truth, and the truth will set you free."*~ John 8:32*

"And whenever you stand praying, forgive, if you have anything against anyone, so that your Father also who is in heaven may forgive you your trespasses." *~Mark 11:25*

"God is not man, that he should lie, or a son of man, that he should change his mind. Has he said, and will he not do it? Or has he spoken, and will he not fulfill it?" *~Numbers 23:19*

"For the word of God is living and active, sharper than any two-edged sword, piercing to the division of soul and of spirit, of joints and of marrow, and discerning the thoughts and intentions of the heart." *~Hebrews 4:12*

*Zeal*

"Those whom I love, I reprove and discipline, so be zealous and repent." *~Revelation 3:19*

"For I bear them witness that they have a zeal for God, but not according to knowledge." *~Romans 10:2*

"Who gave himself for us to redeem us from all lawlessness and to purify for himself a people for his own possession who are zealous for good works." *~Titus 2:14*

"My zeal consumes me, because my foes forget your words." *~Psalm 119:139*

"He put on righteousness as a breastplate, and a helmet of salvation on his head; he put on garments of vengeance for clothing, and wrapped himself in zeal as a cloak." *~Isaiah 59:17*

"So we do not lose heart. Though our outer self is wasting away, our inner self is being renewed day by day. For this light momentary affliction is preparing for us an eternal weight of glory beyond all comparison, as we look not to the things that are seen but to the things that are unseen. For the things that are seen are transient, but the things that are unseen are eternal." *~2 Corinthians 4:16-18*

"For God gave us a spirit not of fear but of power and love and self-control." *~2 Timothy 1:7*

"Not that I seek the gift, but I seek the fruit that increases to your credit." *~Philippians 4:17*

"As for you, brothers, do not grow weary in doing good." *~ 2 Thessalonians 3:13*

"Do not be slothful in zeal, be fervent in spirit, serve the Lord." *~Romans 12:11*

I hope this book inspires you to pursue a life of purpose and passion. I encourage you to create a life that is rooted in being of service to the world. It is my sincerest prayer that the advice, the hashtags, the tweets and the affirmations in this book assist you in claiming a life that is better than the ordinary. From my heart to yours, always remember to

BE Extraordinary